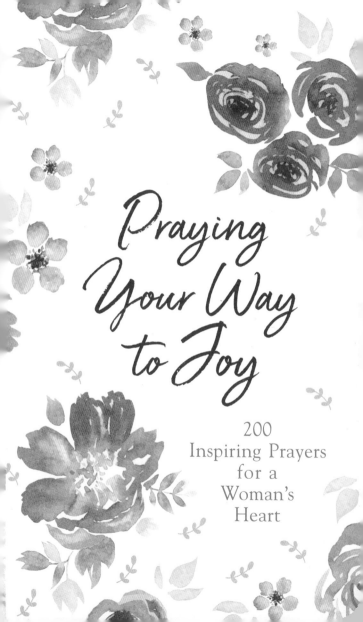

Praying Your Way to Joy

200
Inspiring Prayers
for a
Woman's
Heart

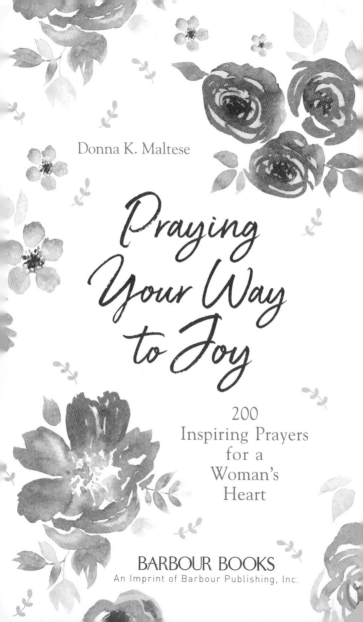

Donna K. Maltese

Praying Your Way to Joy

200
Inspiring Prayers
for a
Woman's
Heart

BARBOUR BOOKS
An Imprint of Barbour Publishing, Inc.

© 2019 by Barbour Publishing, Inc.

ISBN 978-1-64352-193-0

All rights reserved. No part of this publication may be reproduced or transmitted for commercial purposes, except for brief quotations in printed reviews, without written permission of the publisher.

Scripture quotations marked ESV are from The Holy Bible, English Standard Version®, copyright © 2001 by Crossway Bibles, a publishing ministry of Good News Publishers. Used by permission. All rights reserved.

Scripture quotations marked MSG are from *THE MESSAGE*. Copyright © by Eugene H. Peterson 1993, 1994, 1995, 1996, 2000, 2001, 2002. Used by permission of NavPress Publishing Group.

Scripture quotations marked NLV are taken from the New Life Version copyright © 1969 and 2003 by Barbour Publishing, Inc. All rights reserved.

Scripture quotations marked NKJV are taken from the New King James Version®. Copyright © 1982 by Thomas Nelson, Inc. Used by permission. All rights reserved.

Scripture quotations marked AMPC are taken from the Amplified® Bible, Classic Edition © 1954, 1958, 1962, 1964, 1965, 1987 by The Lockman Foundation. Used by permission.

Published by Barbour Books, an imprint of Barbour Publishing, Inc., 1810 Barbour Drive, Uhrichsville, Ohio 44683, www.barbourbooks.com

Our mission is to inspire the world with the life-changing message of the Bible.

Member of the
Evangelical Christian
Publishers Association

Printed in China.

Dipping into God's Strength

*They read from the book of the Law of God,
telling the meaning of it so that they understood
what was read. . . . Ezra said to them, "Go, eat
and drink what you enjoy, and give some to him
who has nothing ready. For this day is holy to
our Lord. Do not be sad for the joy of
the Lord is your strength."*

NEHEMIAH 8:8, 10 NLV

Lord, so many times I find myself trying to live in my own strength, and by the end of the day I come up empty and sad, tired and worn. Yet when I see this passage in Your Book, I realize I've been drawing from the wrong well. So here I am, Lord, coming to You, finding where my true strength lies—in Your joy. I am dipping into Your love, communing with Your Spirit, filling up on the sheer bliss of Your presence. Be with me here and now and throughout this day as I feast on You, share Your blessings with others, and discover Your everlasting joy. Amen.

Even at Night

I will give honor and thanks to the Lord, Who has told me what to do. Yes, even at night my mind teaches me. I have placed the Lord always in front of me. Because He is at my right hand, I will not be moved. And so my heart is glad. My soul is full of joy. My body also will rest without fear.

PSALM 16:7–9 NLV

⟿

You, Lord, are the font of wisdom. You are the One who knows all things—even how many hairs are on my head! So I am giving honor and thanks to You. Show me which way to go, what to say, when to say it. At night, Lord, stop all those what-if thoughts from ricocheting around in my head. Replace them with Your peace and presence. With You next to me, I know nothing can shake me. I can stand in confidence and move forward in hope. You make my heart soar with gladness. You fill my soul with joy. My body relaxes in Your all-encompassing peace as I lean back upon You and rest my weary head. Amen.

All Good Things

Keep me, O God, for I am safe in You.
I said to the Lord, "You are my Lord. All the
good things I have come from You." As for those
in the land who belong to You, they are the
great ones in whom is all my joy.
PSALM 16:1–3 NLV

Lord, when I am alone, scared, or confused, I know I can run to You. You are the One who can protect me from all that comes against me, within and without. In You I can hide from the lure of the world. In You my soul and spirit find peace and calm. You have a way of unruffling my feathers, ever so gently. So now, in this moment, I come to rest in Your companionable light, love, and silence. Place Your hedge of protection around me, sheltering me from outside dangers and inner negative thoughts. Remind me that all the good I have in this life comes from You. Thank You, Lord, for all Your blessings upon me and for all the joy You have waiting for me as I wait on You. "You are my Lord. All the good things I have come from You." In Jesus' name, I pray, amen.

Happiness Forever

My future is in Your hands. The land given to me is good. Yes, my share is beautiful to me. . . . For You will not give me over to the grave. And You will not allow Your Holy One to return to dust. You will show me the way of life. Being with You is to be full of joy. In Your right hand there is happiness forever.

PSALM 16:5–6, 10–11 NLV

❧

Lord, when I'm stuck in a pattern of negative thoughts or am allowing fear to control my life, my heart races, my brow sweats, my soul despairs, and my spirit sinks. And it's all because I've some-how moved away from You; forgotten Your power, grace, mercy, strength, and help. I'm allowing everything *but You* to control me. So I'm back, Lord, remembering *You* are the One who holds my future. *You* are the One who has helped me in the past and given me all the good I have. So here I am in the present in Your presence. Here with You, I find my joy! For I know You will show me the way You would have me go, the way that leads to that happily forever after. Amen.

Keep Asking, Seeking, and Knocking

Keep on asking and it will be given you; keep on seeking and you will find; keep on knocking [reverently] and [the door] will be opened to you. For everyone who keeps on asking receives; and he who keeps on seeking finds; and to him who keeps on knocking, [the door] will be opened.

MATTHEW 7:7–8 AMPC

❦

Just when I'm ready to give up, Lord, You bring scriptures like this to my attention and give me the hope I need to keep coming to You. Through Your Son, Jesus, You've made it clear that if I keep asking, seeking, and knocking, You *will* come through for me. I *will* receive what I'm asking for, find what I seek, and have doors opened to me. So here I am, Lord, asking, seeking, and knocking, knowing You will provide what I desire. And that, if need be, You'll change that desire to better align with Yours. In this and so many other ways, Lord, You revive my hope. Joy begins to warm my heart as my discouragement morphs into encouragement. Thank You for all this and more. I pray in Jesus' name, amen.

Giving Way to God

Do not trouble yourself because of sinful men.
Do not want to be like those who do wrong. For
they will soon dry up like the grass. Like the green
plant they will soon die. Trust in the Lord, and do
good. So you will live in the land and will be fed.
Be happy in the Lord. And He will give you the
desires of your heart. Give your way over to the
Lord. Trust in Him also. And He will do it.
PSALM 37:1–5 NLV

Lord, through Your Word, You have given me
the way to walk the road of joy. First, I'm not to
worry about those who are divisive or seem intent
on doing evil. They will not be around forever.
Instead, I'm to trust in You and do good in this
world. Then I will find all I need to live the life
You have designed for me. Then I will find joy
in You and receive the desires of my heart. So in
this moment, right here, right now, I'm letting
You take control of my life. I'm trusting You for
all, knowing it is in You alone I'll find joy. Amen.

Great Expectations

The Lord [earnestly] waits [expecting, looking,
and longing] to be gracious to you; and therefore
He lifts Himself up, that He may have mercy
on you and show loving-kindness to you. . . .
Blessed (happy, fortunate, to be envied) are
all those who [earnestly] wait for Him, who
expect and look and long for Him [for His victory,
His favor, His love, His peace, His joy, and
His matchless, unbroken companionship]!
ISAIAH 30:18 AMPC

❧

How wonderful, Lord, that in every moment You
are waiting and expecting to be gracious to me.
You have scads of mercy and loving-kindness
whenever I need them. So help me be patient,
Lord. Help me to drop whatever burdens I'm bearing and open up my arms to You and the blessings
You have for me. My eyes are on You. I long for
Your never-ending supply of strength, love, peace,
and joy. I cherish and seek out Your company,
Your "matchless, unbroken companionship," each
and every second of my day. For I know that by
returning to and resting in You, I will be saved.
In quietness and trusting confidence I will find
my Source of strength (see Isaiah 30:15). Amen.

Boldly Believing

If you don't know what you're doing, pray to the
Father. He loves to help. You'll get his help, and
won't be condescended to when you ask for it.
Ask boldly, believingly, without a second thought.
People who "worry their prayers" are like wind-
whipped waves. Don't think you're going to
get anything from the Master that way,
adrift at sea, keeping all your options open.
JAMES 1:5–8 MSG

Lord, I feel as if I'm sinking in a quagmire of con-
fusion. I don't know what to do, where to go, what
to say, how to proceed. Lord, help me. Show me
the way to go, the path to take, the words to say.
I come to You boldly, with no reservations. For
I truly believe You want to help and will choose
the best path for me. And I'm not going to worry
about the answer You give me, wondering how
this will all work out. Instead, I am going to do
whatever You call me to do, knowing that whenever You're involved in my plans, You will give
me what I need to see them through and lead me
to a place of joy in the process. So tell me what to
do, Lord. Speak. Your servant is listening. Amen.

More Than You Need

*Do not trouble yourself when all goes well with
the one who carries out his sinful plans. Stop being
angry. Turn away from fighting. Do not trouble
yourself. It leads only to wrong-doing. For those
who do wrong will be cut off. But those who wait
for the Lord will be given the earth. . . . And they
will be happy and have much more than they need.*

PSALM 37:7–9, 11 NLV

Sometimes, Lord, I get so discouraged. It seems
as if the people who get all the breaks are those
who are *not* followers of You! It's so frustrating.
But then I remember that even those who seem
to have everything actually have nothing—
because they don't have You. So I'm not going
to worry about the ne'er-do-wells. Instead, I'm
going to focus my eyes on You. I'm going to do
good because I know it not only pleases You but
also gives me so much joy. I'm waiting on You,
Lord, following You, loving You, looking to You
for everything. For when I give You my all, I get
Your all. Amen.

A Safe Place

*The steps of a good man are led by the Lord.
And He is happy in his way. When he falls,
he will not be thrown down, because the Lord
holds his hand. . . . For the Lord loves what is
fair and right. He does not leave the people alone
who belong to Him. . . . He. . .saves them,
because they go to Him for a safe place.*

PSALM 37:23–24, 28, 40 NLV

❧

Here's one of the things I love most about You,
Lord. When I follow Your way instead of my
own, I am happy, full of that inner joy only You
can supply, no matter what happens. Because
even if I trip up, You come to my rescue. You
hold my hand and pull me back up on my feet
so I can start all over again. As I grow closer and
closer to You, I know I'm exactly where I belong.
For You promise to always be with me. You will
never leave me alone because I am Your daughter, precious in Your sight. And when things
go dark, when shadows chase me, I run to You,
straight into Your arms, where I am not only safe
but comforted and remade. Amen.

A Grand Plan

*I know the thoughts and plans that I have for you,
says the Lord, thoughts and plans for welfare and
peace and not for evil, to give you hope in your
final outcome. Then you will call upon Me, and
you will come and pray to Me, and I will hear and
heed you. Then you will seek Me, inquire for,
and require Me [as a vital necessity] and find Me
when you search for Me with all your heart.*

JEREMIAH 29:11–13 AMPC

❧

I love that You have a plan for me, Lord. The fact
that You even *think* of me is astounding! Sometimes I feel so lost in this world, as if I'm just one
more bit of dust, unimportant, overlooked. And
then I read in Your Word that if I call on You,
You will bend Your ear to my lips. You'll actually
listen to me, hear what I have to say, and move
to work in my life. If I seek You with my whole
self—my heart, soul, mind, and strength—and
need You in every way, I *will* find You. All this is a
balm for my soul and a boost to my spirit. Amen.

The Secret Place

The Lord is my light and the One Who saves me.
Whom should I fear? The Lord is the strength
of my life. Of whom should I be afraid? . . . In
the day of trouble. . . . In the secret place. . .He
will hide me. He will set me high upon a rock.
Then my head will be lifted up above all those
around me who hate me. I will give gifts
in His holy tent with a loud voice of joy.
PSALM 27:1, 5–6 NLV

Fear can be a major killjoy, but I'm shoring up my confidence in You, Lord. You are the most powerful being in heaven and on earth. So I need not fear anything or anyone who comes against me. You, Lord, are the One who gives me the strength to stand. My faith in You gives me the confidence I need. When the trouble starts, You give me shelter. You keep me from the darkness and warm me with Your light. When I'm in Your secret place, You increase my courage. And it is there that I cry out with joy, praising You with all my heart. Thank You, Lord, for being my all in all. Amen.

Heart Strong

*You have been my Helper. . . . For my father
and my mother have left me. But the Lord will
take care of me. . . . I would have been without
hope if I had not believed that I would see the
loving-kindness of the Lord in the land of the
living. Wait for the Lord. Be strong. Let your
heart be strong. Yes, wait for the Lord.*

PSALM 27:9–10, 13–14 NLV

Sometimes even when I'm surrounded by lots
of people, I can feel all alone. I am out of step
with them because I'm so in step with You, Lord.
Yet strangely enough, it's in those times that I
feel even closer to You. Because I know that no
matter who I lose, I'll always have You. You are
the Helper I crave to be with. You are the One
who has taken care of me in the past, is doing
so in the present, and will continue to do so in
the future. This truth gives me hope and revives
my joy. For I know I'll see Your loving-kindness
here and now. Meanwhile, I wait, knowing that
as I do, You are keeping my heart and spirit
strong. Amen.

Request Granted

*Jabez was honorable above his brothers; but his
mother named him Jabez [sorrow maker], saying,
Because I bore him in pain. Jabez cried to the God
of Israel, saying, Oh, that You would bless me and
enlarge my border, and that Your hand might be
with me, and You would keep me from evil so it
might not hurt me! And God granted his request.*

1 CHRONICLES 4:9–10 AMPC

❧

I thank You, Lord, that You have provided me
with the gift and tool of prayer. No matter how
I am seen or labeled in this world, by praying to
You, I can change the conversation, within and
without. Although my name is not Sorrow Maker,
I ask You, Lord, for Your many blessings. I ask that
You would increase what I already have. That Your
hand would be with me to protect me. That You
would keep me from evil so I am not hurt. That
You would fill my head with good thoughts. That
You would open my mind and heart to Your Word,
allowing it to change me from the inside out for
Your glory alone. In Jesus' name, I pray, amen.

"All Is Well"

She went up and laid [her dead son] on the bed
of the man of God and shut the door behind him
and went out. . . . She said, "All is well.". . .
She set out and came to the man of God. . . .
He said to Gehazi his servant, "Look, there is
the Shunammite. Run at once to meet her and
say to her, 'Is all well with you? Is all well with
your husband? Is all well with the child?' "
And she answered, "All is well."

2 KINGS 4:21, 23–26 ESV

Lord, You Yourself know there is nothing harder in life than losing one's only child. It is heartbreaking. Yet the Shunammite woman had so much faith that even when her child stopped breathing, she knew all would be well. She set her face toward the man of God named Elisha, knowing that through him, You would make everything all right. And You did, bringing her child back to life! Help me, Lord, to have the same attitude no matter what happens in my life, no matter how You answer my prayers. Help me live in and with peace and joy, knowing that with You, all is well and will be well. In Jesus' name, amen.

Strengthened with Trust

The village. . .had been burned to the ground,
and their wives, sons, and daughters all taken
prisoner. David and his men burst out in loud
wails—wept and wept until they were exhausted
with weeping. . . . There was talk among the
men, bitter over the loss of their families, of
stoning him. David strengthened himself with
trust in his GOD. . . . Then David prayed to
GOD. . . . David recovered the whole lot.
1 SAMUEL 30:3–4, 6, 8, 19 MSG

Your Word makes clear, Lord, that there are times
when it's okay to have a good cry. I should take
time to mourn over the losses I suffer in this world.
After all, Jesus cried, so why not me? Yet when
I'm all cried out, I need to seek Your face so I can
find my way out of any why-me conundrums. I
garner strength and encouragement by sitting
in Your presence. Then I am to pray, asking You
what I should do to find a path to restoration.
Only when I have received Your instruction am
I to take the next steps. For only with Your power
can I live out Your plan and be restored to joy
once more. Amen.

Nevertheless

The king and his men went to Jerusalem against the Jebusites, the inhabitants of the land, who said to David, "You will not come in here, but the blind and the lame will ward you off"—thinking, "David cannot come in here." Nevertheless, David took the stronghold of Zion, that is, the city of David. . . . And David became greater and greater, for the LORD, the God of hosts, was with him.

2 SAMUEL 5:6–7, 10 ESV

Every success David had, Lord, was because You were with him—*and* David was with You. That's how I want to live my life, Lord. When You call me to do something, when You want me to follow in Jesus' steps and to live out what You have planned for me, I do not want to be dissuaded or discouraged by what other people say. I want to *nevertheless* take the strongholds You want me to take. Win the battles You want me to win. For then, not only will I have the joy of that success, but You will take joy in me as well. Give me that courage, Lord. Be with me in all You would have me do. Help me to live a nevertheless life for Your glory. Amen.

Saving Power

"The Lord says to you, 'Do not be afraid or troubled because of these many men. For the battle is not yours but God's. Go down to fight them tomorrow. . . . You will not need to fight in this battle. Just stand still in your places and see the saving power of the Lord work for you, O Judah and Jerusalem.' Do not be afraid or troubled. Go out against them tomorrow, for the Lord is with you."

2 Chronicles 20:15–17 NLV

Lord, when forces come up against me, I so often try to fight them on my own, in my own strength, and according to my own game plan. Yet Your Word makes it clear that the very first thing I should do when I'm in trouble is come to You, praising You and thanking You for all the ways You provide for me and work in my life. Then I am to ask what I should do—if I should stand still and watch You fight for me or move out and face my foe with Your strength and courage running through me, knowing that in the end, whatever the result, I *will* rejoice in Your saving power. Amen.

The Power of Praise

"Trust in the Lord your God, and you will be made strong. Trust in the men who speak for Him, and you will do well." . . . [Jehoshaphat] called those who sang to the Lord and those who praised Him in holy clothing. They went out in front of the army and said, "Give thanks to the Lord. For His loving-kindness lasts forever." When they began to sing and praise, the Lord set traps against the men.

2 CHRONICLES 20:20–22 NLV

It's one thing to read about trusting in You, Lord. It's quite another thing to actually *do* the trusting. That's where I sometimes fall short of what and who You want me to be. Help me work on that, Father. Help me to grow stronger and stronger by trusting You. Help me to be the brave woman You created me to be, one who goes out to meet her enemies while she's singing praises to You. It sounds crazy, but I'm trusting You to make this happen and to bring me victory in the process, just as You did for Jehoshaphat and his people who, in the end, "returned to Jerusalem with joy. For the Lord had filled them with joy by saving them" (verse 27). Amen.

Happy for Hope

Now that we have been made right with God by putting our trust in Him, we have peace with Him. It is because of what our Lord Jesus Christ did for us. By putting our trust in God, He has given us His loving-favor and has received us. We are happy for the hope we have of sharing the shining-greatness of God. We are glad for our troubles also. We know that troubles help us learn not to give up.

ROMANS 5:1–3 NLV

Oh Lord Jesus, thank You for loving me so much that You died to save my soul. You did this to make me right with God so that I can have access to Him through prayer and praises. This gives me such peace. It's clear I cannot make it through this life without You by my side, without looking to You for an example of what I am to do and say. Now, as I trust God with all my heart, soul, mind, and strength, I can have joy no matter what my situation. No matter what troubles come against me, I will never give up for I have hope, knowing You will help me through thick and thin, life and death. Amen.

God's Blessings

You shall keep the Feast of Weeks to the Lord your God with a tribute of a freewill offering from your hand, which you shall give to the Lord your God, as the Lord your God blesses you. . . . You shall rejoice in your Feast. . . because the Lord your God will bless you in all your produce and in all the works of your hands, so that you will be altogether joyful.

DEUTERONOMY 16:10, 14–15 AMPC

I can't remember the last time I came to You with nothing but praise and thanks, Lord, for all the ways You've blessed me. Instead, I seem to mostly either unload my troubles or ask You for things. So today, Lord, I come to You wanting nothing, only giving You thanks. Thank You for saving me, loving me, protecting me, and watching over me. Thank You for the food, clothing, and shelter You so adequately provide. Thank You for blessings seen and unseen. And thank You for blessing the work I put my hands to, so that I can be "altogether joyful." What a great God You are! All praise and glory to You, dear Lord. Amen.

Singing and Dancing

David went everywhere that Saul sent him,
and did well. Saul had him lead the men of war.
And it was pleasing to all the people and to Saul's
servants. When David returned from killing the
Philistine, the women came out of all the cities of
Israel, singing and dancing, to meet King Saul,
playing songs of joy on timbrels. The women sang
as they played, and said, "Saul has killed his
thousands, and David his ten thousands."

1 Samuel 18:5–7 nlv

❦

It's so easy to cheer for and celebrate people who play sports or act on the stage or screen. But when it comes to celebrating You, Lord, I seem to hesitate, wondering what people will think of me. Help me to change that up, dear God. I want to be like the women who sang and danced with abandon back in David's day. For doing so not only pleases You but fills me with such joy, lifting me higher in mind, spirit, and body. It's a win-win for both of us, Lord. So I come to You with abandon today, dancing as I sing my song of praise just for You! Amen.

Turned Hearts

They finished their building by decree of the God of Israel and by decree of Cyrus and Darius and Artaxerxes king of Persia. . . . And the people of Israel. . .celebrated the dedication of this house of God with joy. . . . For the LORD had made them joyful and had turned the heart of the king of Assyria to them, so that he aided them in the work of the house of God.

EZRA 6:14, 16, 22 ESV

Only You, Lord, have the power to turn the hearts of rulers, whether they be queens, presidents, tyrants, or dictators, so that Your work can be accomplished through them and us. This gives me hope that You can turn even the most godless person to help Your people do what You have called them to do, no matter how great the task. And that hope in You and Your power working to change people, against all odds and appearances to the contrary, gives me great joy. For with You, nothing is impossible. In Your power I not only rest but go forward with confidence, hope, and joy. In Jesus' name, amen.

Morning Moments

In the morning You hear my voice, O Lord; in the morning I prepare [a prayer, a sacrifice] for You and watch and wait [for You to speak to my heart]. . . . Let all those who take refuge and put their trust in You rejoice; let them ever sing and shout for joy, because You make a covering over them and defend them; let those also who love Your name be joyful in You and be in high spirits.

PSALM 5:3, 11 AMPC

In these early morning moments, Lord, I come to You. Hear my voice. I'm giving You my all—my heart, soul, body, and mind. I await Your presence. Come to me, Lord. Speak gently, softly, to my heart. Tell me the words You want me to hear as I take refuge in You, laying down all my burdens and taking up Your strength, courage, and love. Fill me with Your Spirit. Shield me from any dangers that may come. Help me stay attuned to You all through this day. Lord, I love You ever so much, to the moon and back and more. For it is with and in You that I find my true joy every moment of the day. Amen.

Healing Power

*A gentle tongue [with its healing power] is a
tree of life. . . . A man has joy in making an
apt answer, and a word spoken at the right
moment—how good it is! . . . The mind of the
[uncompromisingly] righteous studies how to
answer. . . . The light in the eyes [of him whose
heart is joyful] rejoices the hearts of others,
and good news nourishes the bones.*
PROVERBS 15:4, 23, 28, 30 AMPC

Lord, please reign over and rein in my tongue.
There are so many times I speak without thinking and end up hurting others. I want to follow
the steps of Christ, Lord—to build people up,
not tear them down. So help me, Lord, to have a
gentle tongue that heals others so they can grow
closer to You. Show me how to increase the joys
of others with a balm, not destroy them with a
bomb. Help me to study how to answer before I
speak and to think before I let one word cross my
lips. For then not only I but those with whom I
speak will be filled with joy. Amen.

A Glad Heart

A glad heart makes a cheerful countenance,
but by sorrow of heart the spirit is broken. . . .
All the days of the desponding and afflicted are
made evil [by anxious thoughts and forebodings],
but he who has a glad heart has a continual feast
[regardless of circumstances]. Better is little with
the reverent, worshipful fear of the Lord than
great and rich treasure and trouble with it.
PROVERBS 15:13, 15–16 AMPC

Abba, some days I find myself brought so low by what's happening in the world. And sometimes my chin is on the floor because of what's happening in my home, my family, or my work. More often than not, my mind is filled with anxious thoughts and forebodings. But I don't want to live that way. I want to have a glad heart—no matter what's happening. So I need Your help to focus on the good things, the things above, not the things of this earth. Help me, Lord, not to worry about anything—money, relationships, wars, or other troubles—but to keep my chin up by keeping my eyes and focus on You alone. In Jesus' name, amen.

In the Arms of the Beloved Shepherd

*Like an apple tree among the trees of the wood,
so is my beloved [shepherd] among the sons [cried
the girl]! Under his shadow I delighted to sit, and
his fruit was sweet to my taste. . . . His banner
over me was love [for love waved as a protecting
and comforting banner over my head when I was
near him]. . . . [I can feel] his left hand under
my head and his right hand embraces me!*

SONG OF SOLOMON 2:3–4, 6 AMPC

Beloved Shepherd, I find more delight, more
joy in Your presence than anywhere else. For
You have told me of Your deep love, which will
never die but continue to protect and comfort
me whenever You are near. So I come to You in
this tender and precious moment. I can feel Your
left hand under my head and Your right hand
pulling me close, into Your loving embrace. As
my head rests against Your breast, I rise and fall
with each of Your breaths. Hold me close, Lord.
Keep me safe as I linger here in Your presence,
safe in body, sound in mind, and happy in heart.
Amen.

Rising Up to the Love

Arise, my love, my fair one, and come away.
[So I went with him, and when we were climbing
the rocky steps up the hillside, my beloved shepherd
said to me] O my dove, [while you are here]. . .
in the sheltered and secret place of the cliff, let me
see your face, let me hear your voice; for your
voice is sweet, and your face is lovely. [My heart
was touched and I fervently sang to him my desire].
SONG OF SOLOMON 2:13–15 AMPC

❧

It fills me with joy, Lord, that You call me "my love." That You want me to come away with You to that secret place where we meet, just You and me alone. That You want to see my face and hear my voice. That You think I'm lovely. Thank You, my Beloved, for calling me to rise up to You and tell You about my desires and all the things that are on my heart. There is nothing and no one like You, Lord. To You alone I bear all my secrets, all my longings, knowing that You will not laugh at them but will treasure them. Dear heart, I love You. Amen.

A Heart Awake

I went to sleep, but my heart stayed awake. [I dreamed that I heard] the voice of my beloved as he knocked [at the door of my mother's cottage]. Open to me, my sister, my love, my dove, my spotless one [he said]. . . . [But weary from a day in the vineyards, I had already sought my rest] I had put off my garment—how could I [again] put it on? I had washed my feet—how could I [again] soil them?

SONG OF SOLOMON 5:2–3 AMPC

Lord, in Your presence I experience such unfathomable joy. Yet at times I am so worn out from earthly cares that I do not open my door to You. In those moments I miss out on Your peace, calm, wisdom, power, strength, and gentle touch. Even in the night hours, asleep or awake, I want to be available to You—to Your voice, Your whisper, Your knock upon my door. Help me keep attuned to Your quest for me. May my spirit be so linked to Yours that I don't know where I stop and You begin. I pray this in Jesus' precious name, amen.

Joyfully Radiant

[She proudly said] I am my beloved's, and his
desire is toward me! . . . Many waters cannot
quench love, neither can floods drown it. . . .
[Joyfully the radiant bride turned to him, the one
altogether lovely, the chief among ten thousand
to her soul, and with unconcealed eagerness to
begin her life of sweet companionship with him,
she answered] Make haste, my beloved, and
come quickly, like a gazelle or a young hart
[and take me to our waiting home].
SONG OF SOLOMON 7:10; 8:7, 14 AMPC

The fact that You desire me, Lord, fills me with such delight. I rejoice that I am Yours and You are mine and that the love we have for each other can never disappear. I am so eager to turn to You, to begin our life together each morning. Take me to that rock that is higher than I, that secret place where it is only You and me, together forever. That is my true home, my true abode where nothing untoward can touch me and where You cover me with Your love. You dry my tears and simply hold me, telling me all is well and will be well. You are my heaven on earth. Amen.

Beyond Understanding

Be full of joy always because you belong to
the Lord. Again I say, be full of joy! Let all
people see how gentle you are. . . . Do not
worry. Learn to pray about everything. Give
thanks to God as you ask Him for what you
need. The peace of God is much greater than
the human mind can understand. This peace will
keep your hearts and minds through Christ Jesus.
PHILIPPIANS 4:4–7 NLV

Joy, at times, seems elusive, Lord. But that's only because I forget to call on You, my Champion, my Master, my Creator, the All-Powerful One who makes the seemingly impossible possible! Instead of running to You, I let my worries begin a running dialogue in my head. Soon they spin out of control and build up to a sort of mild panic. Help me, Lord, to learn to pray about anything and everything—and to thank You in the process. For Your Word says that if I do, Your peace beyond understanding will surround me and guard me. So here I am, Lord, telling You all, thanking You for all. . . . Ah, now it's time to rejoice! Amen.

Humbly Blessed

He opened His mouth and taught them, saying:
Blessed (happy, to be envied, and spiritually
prosperous—with life-joy and satisfaction in God's
favor and salvation, regardless of their outward
conditions) are the poor in spirit (the humble, who
rate themselves insignificant), for theirs is the
kingdom of heaven! . . . [Jesus] poured water into
the washbasin and began to wash the disciples'
feet and to wipe them with the [servant's] towel.
MATTHEW 5:2–3; JOHN 13:5 AMPC

᷅᷅᷅

Jesus, I can't imagine being one of the disciples
whose feet You washed. It seems incomprehen-
sible that You, the Son of God, would kneel before one of Your brothers or sisters and wash his
or her dirty, stinky feet. Yet that's just what You
did—providing the example I am to follow as
Your disciple. Today help me, Lord, to have a
servant's heart and to humble myself, kneeling
before someone who needs my help, no matter
who that person is. For I want to share in Your
joy, to be blessed in and with You, and to gain
the kingdom of heaven! In Your name, amen.

Words of Joy

*O Lord, You know and understand; [earnestly]
remember me and visit me and avenge me on
my persecutors. Take me not away [from joy or
from life itself] in Your long-suffering [to my
enemies]; know that for Your sake I suffer and
bear reproach. Your words were found, and I
ate them; and Your words were to me a joy
and the rejoicing of my heart, for I am called
by Your name, O Lord God of hosts.*

JEREMIAH 15:15–16 AMPC

God, I am so glad You can see what I'm going
through, all the things I'm up against. You know
how my troubles are zapping my joy. But then
I reach for Your Word. I open Your Book and
discover You. Letter by letter, word by word,
sentence by sentence, I absorb all You have to
say to me—how You love and work with me, how
You want all that is good to come to me. You even
have a plan for me. And it is here, within Your
Word and presence, that I find the joy I need
to live this life. Thank You for allowing me to
hear Your voice and find my way home to You.
Amen.

Mind over Matters

*Keep your minds thinking about whatever is true,
whatever is respected, whatever is right, whatever
is pure, whatever can be loved, and whatever is
well thought of. If there is anything good and worth
giving thanks for, think about these things. Keep
on doing all the things you learned and received
and heard from me. Do the things you saw me do.
Then the God Who gives peace will be with you.*
PHILIPPIANS 4:8–9 NLV

Too often, Lord, I find myself so engrossed in the
bad things happening in the world that I forget
about all the good that surrounds me—You and
Your Word included. So help me lift my thoughts
in Your direction, Lord. I want to fill my mind
with and meditate on things that are good, true,
and uplifting. I want to think the best, not the
worst; to think of the lovely, not the unlovely. I
want to think of things to praise, not things to
criticize. But I need Your help. Make it my desire,
Lord, to fill my mind with You before I reach for
the paper or turn on the news. For I know that if
I'm full of You and Your goodness, I won't have
room for anything else—but joy. Amen.

Tender Tears of Love

*He opened His mouth and taught them,
saying: . . . Blessed and enviably happy [with
a happiness produced by the experience of
God's favor and especially conditioned by the
revelation of His matchless grace] are those who
mourn, for they shall be comforted! . . . He
said, Where have you laid him? They said to
Him, Lord, come and see. Jesus wept. The
Jews said, See how [tenderly] He loved him!*
MATTHEW 5:2, 4; JOHN 11:34–36 AMPC

❧

You, Jesus, are well aware of all the sorrows I
have suffered, for You Yourself are called "a
Man of sorrows and pains, and acquainted with
grief" (Isaiah 53:3 AMPC). When You were looking for Your friend Lazarus, knowing he had
died, You wept tears of tender pity and love.
Yet You have taught that even in my sorrows, I
can find joy. For You, who know what I've gone
through, will comfort me. And it is that comfort I seek now. Be with me, Lord. Wipe away
my tears. Hold me in Your arms until I once again
experience gladness in You. Amen.

Glad in God

I'm glad in God, far happier than you would ever guess. . . . I don't have a sense of needing anything personally. I've learned by now to be quite content whatever my circumstances. I'm just as happy with little as with much, with much as with little. I've found the recipe for being happy whether full or hungry, hands full or hands empty. Whatever I have, wherever I am, I can make it through anything in the One who makes me who I am.

PHILIPPIANS 4:10–13 MSG

So many people are miserable, Lord. They are always in a state of wanting, never quite feeling complete and happy. I must admit that sometimes I find myself there too. I am envious of others and what they have and can do. But then I think of You and all those desires fade. I find myself quite content, even happy with what I have and what's happening in my life. For You, Lord, are all I need. With You giving me strength, grace, mercy, love, hope, and so much more, I'm happy whether my pantry is full or empty, my house warm or cold, my bank balance abundant or sparse. I'm at peace and glad in You. Amen.

A Quiet Strength

Blessed (happy, blithesome, joyous, spiritually prosperous—with life-joy and satisfaction in God's favor and salvation, regardless of their outward conditions) are the meek (the mild, patient, long-suffering), for they shall inherit the earth! . . . Say to the Daughter of Zion. . . Behold, your King is coming to you, lowly and riding on a donkey, and on a colt, the foal of a donkey [a beast of burden].

MATTHEW 5:5; 21:5 AMPC

When I think about it, it doesn't seem like I'd be very happy being meek, Jesus. Yet that is what You were and what You've called me to be. When I look to You as my example, I realize being meek doesn't mean being weak. It means being obedient to Abba God. Trusting Him to handle what I cannot. Being quiet and patient while He works out His will and way. And being gentle with others. In this view, being meek carries strength with it. You Yourself, the Son of God and my King, rode a simple donkey through the throng the Sunday before Your death. I want to have that meekness, that trust in Abba God. Show me the way there so that I too can find the joy that comes with quiet strength. Amen.

A Peaceful Sleep

When you are on your bed, look into your hearts and be quiet. Give the gifts that are right and good, and trust in the Lord. Many are asking, "Who will show us any good?" . . . You have filled my heart with more happiness than they have when there is much grain and wine. I will lie down and sleep in peace. O Lord, You alone keep me safe.

PSALM 4:4–8 NLV

It's so hard to have joy, Lord, when I don't get enough sleep at night. So I'm asking for Your help. When I'm in bed, help me commune with my heart. To review my day and ask Your forgiveness for anything I may have done or said that I shouldn't have. To count my blessings, one by one. Then, Lord, help me to quiet my body and soul in Your presence. Fill me with all the joy I need to find peace of heart and mind. For only then, with You and Your blessings covering me, with Your protection and arms around me, will I find the rest I need and the safety I crave. In Jesus' name, I pray, amen.

Spiritual Nourishment

He opened His mouth and taught them, saying: . . .
Blessed and fortunate and happy and spiritually
prosperous (in that state in which the born-again
child of God enjoys His favor and salvation) are
those who hunger and thirst for righteousness
(uprightness and right standing with God), for
they shall be completely satisfied! . . . The disciples
urged Him saying, Rabbi, eat something. But He
assured them, I have food (nourishment) to eat of
which you know nothing and have no idea.
MATTHEW 5:2, 6; JOHN 4:31–32 AMPC

Abba God, only You can fill this longing I have
inside, this God-shaped hole within me. I ache
to hear Your voice, see Your face, feel Your touch.
I hunger and thirst for all You have to give me,
for all You are holding for me. I know You're
just waiting to give me everything I need. So
help me, Lord, to let go of all things that are
not of You—worries, fears, and what-ifs; possessions, deadlines, stress, and anxieties. For when I
empty myself of all but You and Your Word, I
know I'll find the nourishment that brings with
it all the joy my spirit craves. Amen.

Revived Again

*Be to me a rock of refuge, to which I may
continually come. . . . O God, from my youth
you have taught me, and I still proclaim your
wondrous deeds. So even to old age and gray
hairs, O God, do not forsake me, until I
proclaim your might to another generation. . . .
You. . .will revive me again. . . . My lips
will shout for joy, when I sing praises to you.*
PSALM 71:3, 17–18, 20, 23 ESV

You have never failed me, Lord. When I've needed
Your help, You have always come through for me.
Time and time again, You have worked wonders
in my life. Since I was a child in the faith, You
have been my rock of refuge. So do not leave me
now, Lord. Help me to grow more and more like
Your Son, Jesus. Give me the words to tell others
of Your power, love, compassion, and strength.
Renew me. Fill me with Your light. Work in me
for Your good and glory. And I will shout for joy
as I sing Your praises. Amen.

Never Forgotten

Sing for joy, O heavens! Be glad, O earth!
Break out into songs of joy, O mountains!
For the Lord has comforted His people. . . .
"Can a woman forget her nursing child? Can
she have no pity on the son to whom she gave
birth? Even these may forget, but I will not
forget you. See, I have marked your names on
My hands. Your walls are always before Me."
ISAIAH 49:13, 15–16 NLV

Oh Lord, with You in my life, I need not worry
about being passed over! For You are always with
me. You will never forget me—just like a nursing
mother will never forget her newborn. But You
go even further by tattooing my name on Your
hands! Thank You for leading me, protecting me
before and behind, providing for me, healing me,
showering me with blessings, and fighting those
who threaten me. Your pervading presence in my
life gives me such joy. Such peace of mind. Thank
You, Father God, for never leaving me behind.
Because of You, I break out, singing songs of joy.
In Jesus' name, I praise You, amen.

Loving Care Not Spared

He opened His mouth and taught them,
saying: . . . Blessed (happy, to be envied,
and spiritually prosperous—with life-joy and
satisfaction in God's favor and salvation,
regardless of their outward conditions) are the
merciful, for they shall obtain mercy! . . .
As Jesus passed on from there, two blind men
followed Him, shouting loudly, Have pity and
mercy on us, Son of David! . . . Then He
touched their eyes. . .and their eyes were opened.
MATTHEW 5:2, 7; 9:27, 29–30 AMPC

❧

I thank You, Jesus, for Your mercy. Your
loving-kindness and Your care for me seem to
have no end. While You were here on earth, You
were constantly reaching out to help others. And
Your Word tells me that if I am kind and loving
to others, caring for them as You care for me, I
will find myself loved and cared for. So, Lord,
help me to reach out in love to those who need
it. To care for those who are burdened. For when
I do, the blessings and joy will flow, eyes will be
opened, and hearts will be touched for You. In
Jesus' name, amen.

Pure Light and Joy

You are the Lord Most High over all the earth. . . .
Let those who love the Lord hate what is bad.
For He keeps safe the souls of His faithful
ones. He takes them away from the hand of
the sinful. Light is spread like seed for those
who are right and good, and joy for the pure in
heart. Be glad in the Lord, you who are right
and good. Give thanks to His holy name.
PSALM 97:9–12 NLV

Lord, help my love of You keep me away from
things that are not good for me. For anything
that is not good is not of You, God. Keep my
soul safe from the evil that presents itself in the
physical and spiritual worlds. Hide me under Your
banner of love so that the sinful cannot reach me.
Shine Your light along my way so that I will not
stumble upon Your path. Help me to continue
to walk in Jesus' steps, the right and good way,
for there alone will I find the deep joy I seek and
the pure love I crave from You. In Jesus' name,
I pray, amen.

Open Doors

*Though the disciples were behind closed doors
for fear of the Jews, Jesus came and stood among
them and said, Peace to you! So saying, He
showed them His hands and His side. And when
the disciples saw the Lord, they were filled with
joy (delight, exultation, ecstasy, rapture). Then
Jesus said to them again, Peace to you! . . .
And having said this, He breathed on them and
said to them, Receive the Holy Spirit!*

JOHN 20:19–22 AMPC

Lord Jesus, sometimes this world leaves me cowering in fear, afraid to move forward. In defense, I put up walls and barriers, hoping my safety will lie there. But You, Lord, open all doors and come shining through. Your words and Your blessing of peace draw me out of my fear and into You. Seeing Your face, I am filled with joy once more. Reminded of who You are, what You've suffered for me, I am renewed, made whole again. Your peace and Spirit surround me, cocooning me in Your grace, mercy, love, and presence. Breathe on me, Jesus. Strengthen my heart, soul, and mind as I abide and rest in You. Amen.

Blessings of Goodness

The king shall have joy in Your strength, O LORD; and in Your salvation how greatly shall he rejoice! You have given him his heart's desire, and have not withheld the request of his lips. For You meet him with the blessings of goodness. . . . You have made him exceedingly glad with Your presence. For the king trusts in the LORD, and through the mercy of the Most High he shall not be moved.

PSALM 21:1–3, 6–7 NKJV

It's Your strength and power, Lord, that get me through each day, that bring me great joy. Every day You shower me with blessings, giving me what I desire, answering my prayers. All that is good comes from Your hand. And for all these things I thank You, Lord. Yet no blessing, no good thing You place in my life gives me more joy than Your very presence. For it is my trust that You will come when I call, my faith that You are here by my side right now, and my belief in Your loving-kindness that keep me steady, able to walk, able to serve You. In Jesus' name, amen.

Pure Heart Vision

He opened His mouth and taught them, saying:
. . . Blessed (happy, enviably fortunate, and
spiritually prosperous. . .) are the pure in heart,
for they shall see God! . . . No man has ever seen
God at any time; the only unique Son. . .Who is in
the bosom [in the intimate presence] of the Father,
He has declared Him [He has revealed Him and
brought Him out where He can be seen].
MATTHEW 5:2, 8; JOHN 1:18 AMPC

❧

Only by looking at and through You, Jesus, can I see God in all His goodness, strength, power, mercy, and loving-kindness. Yet to be able to see God completely, to actually be able to fully enter into His presence, my heart and mind must be right with You. So help me, Lord, get and keep my heart pure. Help me focus my thoughts on You, Jesus. To steep myself in Your Word. To walk in Your way. To stay on Your path. To forgive as You have forgiven. And to follow Your lead in all I do and say, all I think and pray. In Your name, amen.

Road to Wisdom

Trust in the Lord with all your heart, and do not trust in your own understanding. Agree with Him in all your ways, and He will make your paths straight. Do not be wise in your own eyes. Fear the Lord and turn away from what is sinful. It will be healing to your body and medicine to your bones. . . . Happy is the man who finds wisdom, and the man who gets understanding.

PROVERBS 3:5–8, 13 NLV

❧

This world seems to be getting more and more complicated every day. There are so many choices one can make, so many roads one can take. I'm sometimes confused, Lord, not sure what to do, which path to choose. Give me the wisdom I need to walk the right way. I'm trusting You and Your wisdom, not my own. I'm going to agree with You on everything. I'm turning myself over to You, knowing that in Your wisdom lies my path to true and lasting joy. Under Your direction will I find the true remedy I need. Amen.

Peacemaker and Maintainer

He opened His mouth and taught them,
saying: . . . Blessed (enjoying enviable
happiness, spiritually prosperous—with life-joy
and satisfaction in God's favor and salvation,
regardless of their outward conditions) are the
makers and maintainers of peace, for they shall be
called the sons of God! . . . In Christ Jesus, you
. . .have been brought near. For He is [Himself]
our peace (our bond of unity and harmony).
MATTHEW 5:2, 9; EPHESIANS 2:13–14 AMPC

❧

In this contentious world, Lord, I want to be a
maker and maintainer of peace. To bring harmony
instead of havoc wherever I go, whatever I do,
whomever I meet. But I need help, Lord. Lots of
it. Tell me when to remain silent and when to
speak. And if I am to speak, give me the words
You would have me say. You are my peace, Lord.
Now mold me into someone who can bring peace
to others. When people see the calmness I bear
without, as well as the harmony I keep within,
may they see me as a blessed and happy daughter
of God. In Jesus' name, I pray, amen.

An Eden-Like Transformation

All you who are serious about right living and committed to seeking GOD. Ponder the rock from which you were cut. . . . Abraham, your father, and Sarah, who bore you. Think of it! One solitary man when I called him, but once I blessed him, he multiplied. Likewise I, GOD, will comfort Zion. . . . I'll transform her dead ground into Eden. . .the garden of GOD, a place filled with exuberance and laughter, thankful voices and melodic songs.
ISAIAH 51:1–3 MSG

You, Lord God, can do anything. And You *will* do anything for those serious about living the way You want them to live. To those committed to seeking You each and every day. From Abraham to Jesus, You have blessed Your people by fulfilling their most ardent desires. I want to be as serious about living right as Abraham was. I want to be as committed to seeking You as Jesus was. Then You will turn my world—within and without—into a garden of Eden, a place where laughter is heard, love is spread, and prayers of gratitude roll off our lips. Transform me, Lord, in Jesus' name, amen.

Right for Life

He began to teach them, saying. . ."Those who have it very hard for doing right are happy, because the holy nation of heaven is theirs. You are happy when people act and talk in a bad way to you and make it very hard for you and tell bad things and lies about you because you trust in Me.". . . Christ. . .never sinned and yet He died for us who have sinned. . .so He might bring us to God.

MATTHEW 5:2, 10–11; 1 PETER 3:18 NLV

❧

Lord Jesus, there's no way I can ever repay You for all You've done for me. You who never sinned died so that I, a sinner, might live. You put up with the leers and jeers of the ungodly. You put up with the lies and the pain of unjust accusers. What You've gone through and done for me inspires me, Lord, to take this new life You've given me and live it for You—no matter what others say about me or do to me. Because as I live for You and trust in You, I gain Your kingdom of heaven—and all the joy and happiness that come with it. Thank You, Lord, for bringing me to God. In Your name, I pray, amen.

Looking at You

*"O give thanks to the Lord. Call upon His name.
Let the people know what He has done. Sing to
Him. Sing praises to Him. Tell of all His great
works. Have joy in His holy name. Let the heart of
those who look to the Lord be glad. Look to the Lord
and ask for His strength. Look to Him all the time.
Remember His great works which He has done."*
1 CHRONICLES 16:8–12 NLV

Today, Lord, I want to thank You for calling me.
I praise Your name in remembrance of all You
have done for Your people—from parting the Red
Sea, to making the earth stand still, to sending a
host of angels to protect us, to sending Your Son
to bring us back to You, heart, body, mind, and
soul. You have breathed Your life into me, Lord.
And to You, my Source, I look at all times—for
guidance, protection, love, mercy, forgiveness,
strength, and power. In Your name and works, in
Your lovely face, I find all the joy I desire. Here's
looking at You, Lord, today and forever. Amen.

Never Seen, Yet Believed

*His disciples were again in the house, and Thomas
was with them. Jesus came, though they were
behind closed doors, and stood among them and
said, Peace to you! . . . Because you have seen
Me, Thomas, do you now believe (trust, have
faith)? Blessed and happy and to be envied are
those who have never seen Me and yet have
believed and adhered to and trusted and relied on Me.*

JOHN 20:26, 29 AMPC

It's true, Jesus. I have never seen You physically.
Yet unlike doubting Thomas, I believe in You.
Between You and me are no closed doors. As
soon as You stand beside me, I feel Your peace
and joy, Your strength and power. You call me
blessed and happy because I believe in, rely on,
and trust in You without ever having seen You.
And I *am*! For You are my way to the Father. You
are the truth I need. You are the life I seek. I am
nowhere without You. So stick close to me, Lord,
as I stick close to You. Continually bless me as
I follow in Your footsteps. Help me to recognize
that no matter what each day brings, my path,
my purpose, and my joy lie in You. Amen.

Lifting Up

*I will lift You up, O Lord, for You have lifted
me up. You have not let those who hate me
stand over me in joy. O Lord my God, I cried
to You for help and You healed me. O Lord,
You have brought me up from the grave. You
have kept me alive, so that I will not go down
into the deep. Sing praise to the Lord, all you who
belong to Him. Give thanks to His holy name.*

Psalm 30:1–4 NLV

It's only right that I should lift You up, Lord, because You've certainly lifted me up. When I first
awoke, I wondered what this day would bring.
But before my thoughts went too far, I looked to
You and into Your Word. There I found how You
continually help and heal me. You give me new
life each and every day. You and Your light are
what keep me from sliding into that dark abyss.
So today, Lord, I'm praising Your name, singing songs of love to You. I thank You for always
being there; rescuing me when I'm in danger;
walking with me through the storms; holding me
tight in the night hours; showing me the pathway of life. . .in You. Amen.

Swimming in Success

Simon Peter said to them, "I am going fishing."
The others said, "We will go with you.". . .
That night they caught no fish. Early in the
morning Jesus stood on the shore of the lake. . . .
He said to them, "Put your net over the right
side of the boat. Then you will catch some fish."
They put out the net. They were not able
to pull it in because it was so full of fish. . . .
There were 153 big fish.
JOHN 21:3–4, 6, 11 NLV

Jesus, I love this story of how Your discouraged disciples have caught no fish. Then You come along, tell them what to do, and they end up catching 153! But the best part is that when Peter realizes it's You, he jumps into the water and swims to Your side! What an expression of joy! That's how I feel, Lord. When I'm discouraged, stuck, out of ideas, Your voice comes through. I follow it, and the next thing I know, I'm swimming in success, rushing joyfully to Your side to share my bounty with You! Thank You, Lord, for all the victories You supply, to Your glory. In Jesus' name, I pray, amen.

Dressed with Joy

*Sing praise to the Lord, all you who belong
to Him. . . . His favor is for life. Crying may
last for a night, but joy comes with the new day.
. . . Show me loving-kindness. O Lord, be my
Helper. You have turned my crying into dancing.
You have taken off my clothes made from hair,
and dressed me with joy. So my soul may
sing praise to You, and not be quiet.*
PSALM 30:4–5, 10–12 NLV

Sometimes, Lord, when I'm grieving over a loss,
it's hard to even consider happiness. Yet a seed
of joy can be found in the hope of Your Word.
For You have said, "Crying may last for a night,
but joy comes with the new day." On the down
days, Lord, help me tap into that hope, that
promise that someday, at some point, I will once
again find and experience joy. That You will
turn my crying into dancing, take off my black
mourning suit and dress me with joy. In the meantime, help me write this promise on my heart
so that I can in some way bring this knowledge
to mind when needed and praise You amid the
pain. Amen.

Your Prayer Has Been Heard

The angel said to him, "Zacharias, do not be afraid. Your prayer has been heard. Your wife Elizabeth will give birth to a son. You are to name him John. You will be glad and have much joy. Many people will be happy because he is born. He will be great in the sight of the Lord. . . . Even from his birth, he will be filled with the Holy Spirit."

LUKE 1:13–15 NLV

❧

I love Your Word, Lord. For it not only gives me a great picture of You, but its stories prove that You are forever working in people's lives. That You *do* answer prayer. That I should never give up praying for something. No matter how many years go by. No matter how old I get. No matter how seemingly impossible my request becomes. I will never lose hope nor forget that You hear me when I pray. So here I am, Lord, once more coming to You with the same request. Give me the joy of Your answer, Lord. I await Your reply, praising Your name, knowing my prayer has been heard by the Doer of the Impossible. Amen.

Trees of the Woods

"The Lord made the heavens. Honor and great power are with Him. Strength and joy are in His place. . . . Let the heavens be glad. Let the earth be filled with joy. And let them say among the nations, 'The Lord rules!' Let the sea thunder, and all that is in it. Let the field be happy, and all that is in it. Then the trees of the woods will sing for joy before the Lord."

1 CHRONICLES 16:26–27, 31–33 NLV

What joy I find in the idea, in the fact that *You* are the Grand Creator, Lord. That all I see—and all I do not see—has been made by Your hands. You are so great, powerful, and wonderful. All the strength and joy are where You are, and You are everywhere—even inside me as I abide in You. So I am rejoicing in that today, Lord. I trust in You, knowing You are in charge, controlling all things—places, people, and events! What a wonderful world You've created, one in which even the trees sing for joy before You! Be with me in this moment, Lord, as I take a nature walk and bask in the joy of Your making. Amen.

Blessed Belief

[Elizabeth] exclaimed. . . .Blessed (happy, to be envied) is she who believed that there would be a fulfillment of the things that were spoken to her from the Lord. And Mary said, My soul magnifies and extols the Lord, and my spirit rejoices in God my Savior, for He has looked upon the low station and humiliation of His handmaiden. . . . For He Who is almighty has done great things for me.

LUKE 1:42, 45–49 AMPC

I find my strength and joy, Lord, when I believe that You will do what Your Word says, when I have faith that You will keep Your promises to those who love You. Help me build up that belief and faith, Lord, more and more each day. Remind me each and every moment that through Your Word, strength, and power, I will not just find my way through this life, but my soul and spirit will rejoice over You in good times and not-so-good times. Help me base my life on the fact that You are doing great things for me and in me. In Jesus' name and power, I pray, amen.

The Way to Wisdom

Happy is the man who finds wisdom, and the man who gets understanding. . . . She is worth more than stones of great worth. Nothing you can wish for compares with her. Long life is in her right hand. Riches and honor are in her left hand. Her ways are pleasing, and all her paths are peace. . . . Happy are all who hold her near.
PROVERBS 3:13–18 NLV

I want to search out Your knowledge, Lord. To understand what You want me to do, say, and think. Show me the path toward Your wisdom. May I pray for that more than anything else. For that is where I will find my direction. That is where I will find the answers I need. That is where I will discover the way You want me to go. So guide my reading of Your Word today, Lord. Show me what You want me to see. Tell me what You'd have me memorize and write upon my heart. Equip me with all I need to know so I can best serve You and find joy along the way. In Jesus' name, I pray, amen.

Starstruck

The star [the wise men] had seen in the East went before them. It came and stopped over the place where the young Child was. When they saw the star, they were filled with much joy. They went into the house and found the young Child with Mary, His mother. Then they got down before Him and worshiped Him. They opened their bags of riches and gave Him gifts. . . . Then God spoke to them.

MATTHEW 2:9–12 NLV

Jesus, I, like the wise men, followed the light and found You. What joy I discovered in You at our first meeting! What a journey it has been. What wonder I experience each day when I get down on my knees and worship You. I offer You my life, heart, body, mind, and soul. Yet if there are other gifts You would like me to hand over to You or share with others, please show me what they are. For my journey with You has just begun. I want to be Your hands and feet, serving You until I am with You on the other side. Speak to me, Lord. Show me the way to grow ever closer to You. In Your name, I pray, amen.

Fresh Start

Count yourself lucky, how happy you must be—
you get a fresh start, your slate's wiped clean.
Count yourself lucky—GOD holds nothing against
you and you're holding nothing back from him.
When I kept it all inside, my bones turned to
powder, my words became daylong groans. . . .
Then I let it all out; I said, "I'll make a clean breast
of my failures to GOD." Suddenly the pressure was
gone—my guilt dissolved, my sin disappeared.

PSALM 32:1–3, 5 MSG

Lord, when I keep things from You, when I don't
admit to You (or myself) that I've done something wrong, it eats me up inside. One wrongdoing
piles up onto another and another and before
I know it, I feel like I'm about to implode. So
here I am today, Lord, telling You not just the
good things I've done but the not-so-good. And
I ask Your forgiveness in the process. For then
I will once again be able to tap into joy, happy
in God, counting myself lucky in the Lord who
not only removes my sin and guilt but makes
them disappear—forever! What a relief! In Jesus'
name, amen.

The Getaway

*"Are you tired? Worn out? Burned out on religion?
Come to me. Get away with me and you'll recover
your life. I'll show you how to take a real rest.
Walk with me and work with me—watch how I do
it. Learn the unforced rhythms of grace. I won't lay
anything heavy or ill-fitting on you. Keep company
with me and you'll learn to live freely and lightly."*

MATTHEW 11:28–30 MSG

❧

Lord Jesus, joy is elusive at best when I'm not
getting the rest I need—spiritually, mentally,
emotionally, and physically. I'm worn out, burned
out, and just plain tired. Exhausted. So I'm not
just coming to You but limping to You. Please take
this load of cares, worries, and woes off my back.
Help me to give them up, to lay them at Your
feet. Show me how to really rest. Teach me how
to keep pace with and work with You. Help me
walk in the "unforced rhythms of grace." Teach
me how to live this life freely yet more fully. To
bear Your light load so I may once more find joy.
In Your name, amen.

Grounded in the Word

The seed which fell between rocks is like the person who receives the Word with joy as soon as he hears it. Its root is not deep and it does not last long. When troubles and suffering come because of the Word, he gives up and falls away. . . . The seed which fell on good ground is like the one who hears the Word and understands it. He gives much grain.

MATTHEW 13:20–21, 23 NLV

I am so glad, Lord, that at first hearing, I not only took in Your Word with joy but let it take root deep within me. But now sometimes on especially busy days, I find myself not making digging into Your Word a priority. Help me to change that, Lord. To look to You and Your Word before my day begins, before my feet hit the floor. Help me to go deeper and deeper into what You have to say. And help me grow in my prayer life. For I want to be one of Your good and faithful servants. To be so fruitful that I please You more than anyone or anything else, including myself. Amen.

A Hiding Place

*Let all who are God-like pray to You while
You may be found, because in the floods of
much water, they will not touch him. You
are my hiding place. You keep me safe from
trouble. . . . Many are the sorrows of the
sinful. But loving-kindness will be all around
the man who trusts in the Lord. Be glad in the
Lord and be full of joy, you who are right with God!*
PSALM 32:6–7, 10–11 NLV

❧

I am always amazed, Lord, at how You keep me
out of troubles seen and unseen. With You next
to me, above me, below me, behind me, before
me, and within me, I find I am truly safe no matter
what comes my way. You, Lord, are my hiding
place. To You I run. In You I trust. Surround me
not only with Your power, strength, and presence
but with all Your unfathomable loving-kindness
as I praise You and pray to You. Keep my feet
upon Your good path. And in You I will find not
only joy but everything I need. In Jesus' name,
amen.

God-Given Joy

*There is nothing better for a man than to eat
and drink and find joy in his work. I have seen
that this also is from the hand of God. For who
can. . .find joy without Him? For God has given
wisdom and much learning and joy to the person
who is good in God's eyes. But to the sinner He
has given the work of. . .getting many riches
together to give to the one who pleases God.*

ECCLESIASTES 2:24–26 NLV

Lord, some days I find myself not enjoying anything. But now I realize that's because my thoughts
and focus are not on You. For only when I seek
You first and bring You to mind throughout my
day do I find the joy I crave. So remind me of Your
presence, Lord, as I eat and drink. And especially
as I work. For I'm not really working for my boss,
my family, my church, my spouse, or my school.
No, I'm working for You. You are my source of
true joy. All I do, I do for You alone. For that
work is truly what lasts forever and ever. I pray
and praise in Jesus' name, amen.

Giving Cheerfully

He who sows sparingly will also reap sparingly,
and he who sows bountifully will also reap
bountifully. So let each one give as he purposes
in his heart, not grudgingly or of necessity; for
God loves a cheerful giver. And God is able to
make all grace abound toward you, that you,
always having all sufficiency in all things, may
have an abundance for every good work.

2 Corinthians 9:6–8 nkjv

❧

When things are difficult financially, Lord, it's hard to give with a cheerful heart. But then I remember Your law: those who give little will get little, but those who give much will get much. So help me keep that in mind, knowing that when I give cheerfully, no matter what my circumstances, I will reap cheerfully, beginning with a bountiful crop of joy. And I will also reap contentment. For as I give, You promise to supply me with everything I might need for all the work I'm doing in and for You. Ah, what a relief to live with the knowledge that as I bless others, I can count on You blessing me. Thank You, God, for all this and so much more. Amen.

Grand Plans

Sing for joy in the Lord, you who are right
with Him. . . . For the Word of the Lord is right.
He is faithful in all He does. . . . Honor Him.
For He spoke, and it was done. He spoke with
strong words, and it stood strong. . . . The plans
of the Lord stand forever. . . . Happy are the
people He has chosen for His own.
PSALM 33:1, 4, 8–9, 11–12 NLV

Your Word is amazing, Father God. Your plans
never fail. Your promises are sure and certain.
You speak and it is done. You said, "Let there be
light," and there was light. Help me, Lord, to trust
both You and Your Word. To do as You would
have me do. Help me not to be discouraged when
things don't go the way I planned. Remind me
that *You* are the Master Planner and that *I can
trust* in Your plans. As I abide by Your Word, continually strengthened, guided, and empowered, I
find the joy You have waiting for me. For I, Your
chosen daughter, rest upon Your promises. Thank
You, Father God. Amen.

A Faithful Servant

*Master, you entrusted to me five talents; see,
here I have gained five talents more. His master
said to him, Well done, you upright (honorable,
admirable) and faithful servant! You have been
faithful and trustworthy over a little; I will put you
in charge of much. Enter into and share the joy (the
delight, the blessedness) which your master enjoys.*

MATTHEW 25:20–21 AMPC

❧

I want to be a good servant for You, Lord. I want
to use the things with which You have gifted me,
not hide them. So, dear Lord, give me the courage
I need to step out for You. Help me nurture the
talents You've given me then use them for the
good of others and for Your glory. Show me what
You would have me do, what You would want
me to use to benefit Your kingdom. Help me to
be faithful with what You have provided. I long
for the day when we meet face-to-face. The day
when You open Your arms to me and say, "Well
done, My faithful daughter. Come to Me and share
the joy and blessings waiting for you." Amen.

A Time for Everything

*For everything there is a season, and a time
for every matter under heaven: a time to be
born, and a time to die; a time to plant, and a
time to pluck up what is planted; a time to kill,
and a time to heal; a time to break down, and a
time to build up; a time to weep, and a time to
laugh; a time to mourn, and a time to dance.*

ECCLESIASTES 3:1–4 ESV

Your Word, Lord, tells me there's a time for everything that happens—life and death, planting and sowing, weeping and laughing, mourning and dancing. And that's just the beginning of Your list. But I get it, Lord. I know some days I'll be sick, praying for Your healing touch. Other days I may be mourning, seeking Your comfort. But through all these seasons, Lord, help me to maintain an undercurrent of Your joy, no matter what my day brings. Help me to realize that someday all these seasons will pass. In the meantime, I can develop into the woman you created me to be and dip into Your stream of joy, because I have my hope in heaven with You. Amen.

Help and Shield

No king is saved by the power of his strong army.
A soldier is not saved by great strength. A horse
cannot be trusted to win a battle. Its great strength
cannot save anyone. . . . Our soul waits for the
Lord. He is our help and our safe cover. For our
heart is full of joy in Him, because we trust in His
holy name. O Lord, let Your loving-kindness be
upon us as we put our hope in You.
PSALM 33:16–17, 20–22 NLV

Lord, sometimes I grow impatient. Instead of waiting for You to move, I find myself trusting in something *other* than You to save me. I begin to scheme, to make plans, to search for my own solutions. Yet those ideas never seem to work, and I just muck things up even more, within and without. I realize I cannot rely on anyone's strength but Yours, Lord. So please give me the gift of patience. Help me to wait on You, my Help and Shield, knowing that You've got everything under control. Your timing is the best. As I put my hope in You alone, my heart fills with joy. For You will work all things out for my good, here and beyond. Amen.

Hidden Treasure

God's kingdom is like a treasure hidden in a field for years and then accidentally found by a trespasser. The finder is ecstatic—what a find!—and proceeds to sell everything he owns to raise money and buy that field. Or, God's kingdom is like a jewel merchant on the hunt for excellent pearls. Finding one that is flawless, he immediately sells everything and buys it.

MATTHEW 13:44–46 MSG

I know my only path to joy, Lord Jesus, is to sacrifice all that I am and have so that I can gain Your kingdom. Through You, I can reach out to Father God, tap into His power, gain His blessing, get the guidance I need to do as He bids, and so much more. So help me, Jesus, to put You above all things. To seek You before all else. To turn to You upon waking in the morning and then just before I turn out the light at night. For the only joy upon earth is to be focused upon You in heaven. To be in Your presence, feel Your embrace, and be showered by Your love and kindness. What a treasure! What a find! In Your name, I pray and rejoice. Amen.

Valley of Blessing

Jehoshaphat and his people came to take away what they wanted. . .more than they could carry. . . . It took them three days to take all the things, because there was so much. They gathered together in the Valley of Beracah [blessing] on the fourth day. There they praised and thanked the Lord. . . . They returned to Jerusalem with joy. For the Lord had filled them with joy by saving them.

2 CHRONICLES 20:25–27 NLV

❧

How wonderful to know, Lord, that when I'm in trouble and I lay my problem before You, ask for Your advice, and vow to do as You say, You move into action. You turn what seem like impossible situations into amazing victories. You turn curses into blessings. When I pray, You do things beyond my imagining. For there is nothing You cannot do. No problem You cannot fix. No curse You cannot reverse. And before I know it, I find myself in the Valley of Blessing. Thank You, Lord, for not just saving me but championing me. For answering not just one prayer but thousands. For working in my life and filling me with irrepressible joy in You. Amen.

Seeking Jesus

*Mary Magdalene and the other Mary went
to see the tomb. . . . The angel said to the
women, "Do not be afraid, for I know that
you seek Jesus. . . . He is going before you to
"Galilee; there you will see him.". . . They
departed quickly from the tomb with fear and
great joy. . . . And behold, Jesus met them and
said, "Greetings!" And they. . .worshiped him.*
MATTHEW 28:1, 5, 7–9 ESV

❧

Like the Marys, I too, Lord, am a female disciple.
As such, I want to be as faithful to You as they
were. Without fear, I look for You. With faith, I
find You. And I'm never going to let You go. Be
with me now. Help me look beyond myself and
my assumptions and look to You and Your truth.
I want to walk in Your will and way. To hear
Your voice speak. To tell others where they can
find You, what they can tell You, and how You
will appear at the sound of our plea and prayer.
Knowing that each day I can and will see You fills
me with joy as I bow down at Your feet, ready to
worship, to listen, to serve. In Your name, amen.

My God, My Help

O send out Your light and Your truth, let them
lead me. . .to Your dwelling. Then will I go to
the altar of God, to God, my exceeding joy. . . .
Why are you cast down, O my inner self?
And why should you. . .be disquieted within me?
Hope in God and wait expectantly for Him,
for I shall yet praise Him, Who is the help of
my [sad] countenance, and my God.
PSALM 43:3–5 AMPC

❦

Lord, I come to Your Word. Send Your light out to me. Allow it to reveal the truth You would have me know. Let the light of Your Word lead me into Your presence, the place where I find my peace, feel Your touch, and experience unfathomable joy. Calm my soul, Lord. Erase my anxiety. Be the balm to my inner self. Renew my hope, Lord. Help me to wait for You, to expect Your goodness to meet my prayer. Give me these moments of quiet. Make my spirit as calm as still water. And as I rest here with You, I give You all my praise and the joy that comes with it. Amen.

A Great Light

Gloom will not be upon her who is distressed. . . .
The people who walked in darkness have seen a
great light. . . . Upon them a light has shined. . . .
They rejoice before You. . . . For unto us a Child
is born, unto us a Son is given. . . . And His name
will be called Wonderful, Counselor, Mighty God,
Everlasting Father, Prince of Peace.
ISAIAH 9:1–3, 6 NKJV

When the shadows of sadness come upon me,
Lord, rise up. Shine Your light down upon me.
Break up the gloom that threatens to envelop
me. Expel the darkness so that I may rejoice in
Your Son-shine. You are the wonder of my life.
You have the guidance I need to walk Your way.
Deliver me with Your mighty power. Counsel
me with Your wisdom. Let no one snatch me out
of Your hand. Be my forever Father, my Shield,
my Protector, my Abba God. Be the priceless
Prince with whom I live happily ever after in
this world and the next. Lord, surround me with
Your peace, love, grace, and mercy as I abide in
You. In Jesus' name, amen.

Eye-Opener

*They began to recognize God and praise and give
thanks. . . . God has visited His people [in
order to help and care for and provide for them]!
And this report concerning [Jesus] spread. . . .
In that very hour Jesus was healing many [people]
of sicknesses and distressing bodily plagues and evil
spirits, and to many who were blind He gave
[a free, gracious, joy-giving gift of] sight.*
LUKE 7:16–17, 21 AMPC

❧

I am still amazed, Father God, by the gift You
have given me in Your Son, Jesus. Through Him,
You came and walked among us. You are and
have been my Helper, Caretaker, and Provider.
You heal me from the sickness within my body,
mind, spirit, and soul. You de-stress me, taking
away my cares, woes, anxieties, and issues. You
have opened my eyes to the truth of Your Word.
Through that lens, I see the path You want me
to take, the road You want me to travel. Thank
You for the joy-giving gift of Jesus, the One who
continually opens my eyes, mind, and heart so
that I can see You. In His name, I pray, amen.

Good Words

*Lying is in the heart of those who plan what is
bad, but those who plan peace have joy. . . .
The Lord hates lying lips, but those who speak
the truth are His joy. . . . Worry in the heart of
a man weighs it down, but a good word makes it
glad. . . . Life is in the way of those who are right
with God, and in its path there is no death.*
PROVERBS 12:20, 22, 25, 28 NLV

You, Lord, are the Master of Truth and the arch-
enemy of the father of lies. So, Lord, help me be
very aware of all the words I allow to leave my
lips. Keep me on the path of truth so that I will
be a person who makes plans for peace. For I want
to please You and partake of all the joy that
offers. I realize worries are nothing more than lies
I tell myself. They imply that I don't trust You.
So filter my words, Lord. Keep any and all
untruths from my mind and lips because my
desire is to be right with You in thought, word,
and deed. Amen.

Good News

There were shepherds in the fields. . .watching their
flocks of sheep at night. The angel of the Lord came
to them. The shining-greatness of the Lord shone
around them. They were very much afraid. The
angel said to them, "Do not be afraid. See! I bring
you good news of great joy which is for all people.
Today, One Who saves from the punishment of sin
has been born. . . . He is Christ the Lord."
LUKE 2:8–11 NLV

❧

I love how You gave Your Son's birth announce-
ment to humankind, Lord. You directed angels
to proclaim the great news, the Good News,
about Jesus to a simple band of shepherds, socially
considered one of the lowest groups of people.
The angel's first words to them were, "Don't be
afraid. I've got some good news that's going to
bring you great happiness. Jesus, God's Son, will
save you!" When *I* first heard Your news, it seemed
too good to be true—that someone sacrificed all
so that I could live for You, see You, pray to You.
Yet that good news was, still is, and forever will
be true. Thank You for the joy I find in Jesus,
Your Son and my Lord, King, and Savior. Amen.

The Voice of Joy

Show your happiness, all peoples! Call out to God with the voice of joy! For the Lord Most High is to be feared. He is a great King over all the earth. He sets people under us, and nations under our feet. He chooses for us what is to be ours, the pride of Jacob, whom He loves. . . . God rules over the nations. God sits on His holy throne.

PSALM 47:1–4, 8 NLV

❧

It seems so easy, Lord, for me to get weighed down by world news. I sometimes feel so helpless, unable to stop the tide of evil. Yet that's not how You would have me be. For I'm Your child. You're my King, the One who rules over all things, who chooses what I am to be and have in this life. You want me to be filled with joy. For what kind of witness would I be for You if I were constantly worried, frightened, upset, and anxious? So, Lord, today, right here, right now, turn my frown upside down! Give me that deep sense of joy from which I can draw—no matter what's happening within and without. In Jesus' name, I pray and praise, amen.

The Habit of Joyful Hope

*Let us. . .rejoice in our sufferings, knowing
that pressure and affliction and hardship
produce patient and unswerving endurance.
And endurance (fortitude) develops maturity of
character (approved faith and tried integrity).
And character [of this sort] produces [the habit of]
joyful and confident hope of eternal salvation. Such
hope never disappoints or deludes or shames us,
for God's love has been poured out in our hearts
through the Holy Spirit Who has been given to us.*
ROMANS 5:3–5 AMPC

❧

Even when I feel as if I'm going through the
wringer, Lord, I have hope. For Your Word tells
me that my troubles are actually good for me. They
strengthen me. They bring me back to You. They
remind me of the joy I have because I know I will
one day be with You in heaven forever. And it is
that hope that keeps me going, looking to You,
feeling Your love bloom within me through the
Holy Spirit You've given me. Within You, Lord, I
have all I need not just to get through this life but
to experience Your abundant peace and provision
amid the process. Amen.

A Forever Guide

*Fair and beautiful in elevation, is the joy of
all the earth—Mount Zion [the City of
David]. . . . God has made Himself known
in her palaces as a Refuge (a High Tower and
a Stronghold). . . . We have thought of Your
steadfast love, O God, in the midst of Your
temple. . . . For this God is our God forever and
ever; He will be our guide [even] until death.*
PSALM 48:2–3, 9, 14 AMPC

It's hard to imagine, Lord, that You chose me as
Your vessel. My fragile body is Your amazing temple. Therein You guide, love, help, and strengthen
me. You have made Yourself known to me as a
Refuge. To You I run, knowing You will shield me
in Your High Tower. You will defend me, for You
are my supernatural Stronghold. And in the midst
of all this, I am overwhelmed by Your lavish love.
You are mine and I am Yours forever and ever.
Continue, Lord, to fill me with Your joy. To be
my Guide here and now, and even to death and
beyond. In Jesus' name, I pray, amen.

Occupied with Joy

What I have seen to be good and fitting is to eat and drink and find enjoyment in all the toil with which one toils under the sun the few days of his life that God has given him, for this is his lot. Everyone also to whom God has given wealth and possessions and power to enjoy them, and to accept his lot and rejoice in his toil—this is the gift of God. For he will not much remember the days of his life because God keeps him occupied with joy in his heart.

ECCLESIASTES 5:18–20 ESV

This is what I want, Lord. To enjoy the life You have given me. To enjoy whatever I eat and drink and whatever work I put my hand to. For this is the life with which You have so wonderfully blessed me. I want to be so focused on all the good things in my life, so content with what You have gifted me, that I don't get hung up on the negative things. I don't want to allow the world's woes to put a shadow upon my blessings from You. Keep me occupied, Lord, with all the joy You have already planted in my heart, today and every day. Amen.

The Agenda for Rejoicing

Jesus said. . . "See what I've given you? Safe passage as you walk on snakes and scorpions, and protection from every assault of the Enemy. No one can put a hand on you. All the same, the great triumph is not in your authority over evil, but in God's authority over you and presence with you. Not what you do for God but what God does for you—that's the agenda for rejoicing."

LUKE 10:19–20 MSG

You have provided me with so many blessings, Jesus, it's hard to count them all. You give me safe passage through this life. Because I live in You, nothing can ever really touch me. No power can ever get through because You're busy protecting me. In fact, no one can even take me out of Your hand! But that's not where my real triumph is. My real triumph is Abba God's power over me and His presence within me. It's not about what I do for God, how He works through me. No. My real cause for rejoicing is all about what He does for me! Thank You, Jesus, for all the blessings You so readily give me and all the ways You work in my life. Amen.

Open Minds

At that, Jesus rejoiced, exuberant in the Holy Spirit. "I thank you, Father, Master of heaven and earth, that you hid these things from the know-it-alls and showed them to these innocent newcomers. Yes, Father, it pleased you to do it this way." . . . He then turned in a private aside to his disciples. "Fortunate the eyes that see what you're seeing. . .to hear what you are hearing."

LUKE 10:21, 23 MSG

Your Word is so precious to me, Lord. The fact that I can pick up my Bible and read about You is amazing. Once I too was a vast wasteland. And then You and Your Word hovered over me. You said, "Let there be light," and I saw the truth for the first time. I heard Your voice speak deep into my spirit. Help me never take for granted the fact that through Your Word I can see how You have been moving. Thank You for letting me read, see, and hear Your story from Genesis to Revelation; for opening my simple mind to the power of Your Word. Every page I turn, every passage I read, prompts me to rejoice in spirit, soul, mind, and heart. Amen.

Lost and Found

"What woman, having ten silver coins, if she loses one coin, does not light a lamp, sweep the house, and search carefully until she finds it? And when she has found it, she calls her friends and neighbors together, saying, 'Rejoice with me, for I have found the piece which I lost!' Likewise, I say to you, there is joy in the presence of the angels of God over one sinner who repents."

LUKE 15:8–10 NKJV

❧

Lord, through Your Word I realize I can, with Your help, bring joy not only to others but to You and Your angels. I know there are many people out there, many sheep who have yet to find You, the Good Shepherd. Yet I also know that You can use me to find them. To be the light that attracts them to You. So help me, Lord, to be that light. To allow Your love and joy to shine through me so powerfully that others will want what I have—You. To that end, I pray, Lord, that Your Holy Spirit would lead the way. That He would use me to turn nonbelievers to You. And that Your angels would then share in the joy of a lost sheep found. In Jesus' name, amen.

A Quenched Thirst

*O God, You are my God. I will look for You with
all my heart and strength. My soul is thirsty for You.
My flesh is weak wanting You in a dry and tired
land where there is no water. . . . I have seen Your
power and Your shining-greatness. . . . I will lift up
my hands in Your name. My soul will be filled. . . .
And my mouth praises You with lips of joy.*

PSALM 63:1–2, 4–5 NLV

❧

Oh Lord, my God, I need You. I need Your presence, Your cooling shade, Your warming arms.
You are everything I desire and thirst for. I am
desperate for Your comfort and love. Give me
some good news through Your Word. Show me
Your power and might. Imbue me with Your love
and grace. Draw me out of myself and into Your
presence. For here alone do I find my Source,
my Provision, my Strength, my Refuge. In You I
am home. In You I have hope. I'm lifting up my
hands, Lord, to praise and worship You. Fill my
soul with Your Spirit. And my mouth will respond
with praises of joy. In Jesus' name, amen.

Moved with Compassion

When he came to himself, he said. . .I will
get up and go to my father, and I will say to him,
Father, I have sinned. . . . While he was still a
long way off, his father saw him and was moved
with pity and tenderness [for him]; and he ran
and embraced him and kissed him [fervently]. . . .
The father said. . .Let us revel and feast
and be happy and make merry.
LUKE 15:17–18, 20, 22–23 AMPC

Sometimes, Lord, I don't realize how far I have
strayed from You. But then when I come to myself,
I know what I have to say. I have to tell You, in
my own words, how I have erred and made a mis-
step. Help me right here and now to ask for Your
forgiveness. Help me to picture You as a Father
who is looking for me, waiting for me, even when
I'm still a long way off. Let me see You as a Father
who is moved with love and compassion for me.
Open Your arms, Lord, as I turn this corner and
run into Your embrace. Grant me Your forgiveness. And may we end this moment by reveling
in each other's company, full of joy, feasting on
our mutual love. Amen.

At Home in God

Silence is praise to you, Zion-dwelling God,
and also obedience. You hear the prayer in it all.
We all arrive at your doorstep sooner or later,
loaded with guilt, our sins too much for us—but
you get rid of them once and for all. Blessed are the
chosen! Blessed the guest at home in your place!
We expect our fill of good things in your house,
your heavenly manse. . . . Dawn and dusk take
turns calling, "Come and worship."
PSALM 65:1–4, 8 MSG

In the stillness of this moment, Lord, I come
before You in silent wonder of who You are, what
You have done, and how You have worked in my
life. Hear my prayer, Lord, as my lips praise You.
Free me of the missteps, the mistakes I have made,
the guilt that weighs me down. Lord, cleanse
me of all shadows. Leave only Your light behind
and within me. Here, in Your presence, I feel I
am home. Thank You for opening Your door to
me. For choosing me, saving me, and loving me.
What joy I find within Your heavenly dwelling,
my Provider, my God. Here I find all I need. Here,
at Your feet, I worship. In Jesus' name, amen.

Seekers

Zacchaeus. . . .was a chief tax collector and was rich. And he was seeking to see who Jesus was, but on account of the crowd he could not. . . . So he ran on ahead and climbed up into a sycamore tree to see him. . . . When Jesus came to the place, he looked up and said to him, "Zacchaeus, hurry and come down, for I must stay at your house today." So he hurried and came down and received him joyfully.

LUKE 19:2–6 ESV

Rich or poor, large or small, Lord, may I always run to catch sight of You. May I not let crowds or distance dissuade me from finding You. You, Lord Jesus, know all who seek Your face. You know our names, stories, conditions. And still You call us to Yourself, telling us to speedily welcome You into our homes, our hearts. And all who do, all who truly want to see Your face, just as they are, Lord, those are the ones with whom You spend time. Those are the ones You save. Those are the ones who revel in the joy of Your presence. Speak to me, Lord. Just as I am. In You, I pray, amen.

Whiter Than Snow

O God, favor me because of Your loving-kindness. Take away my wrong-doing because of the greatness of Your loving-pity. . . . I have sinned against You, and You only. . . . Take away my sin, and I will be clean. Wash me, and I will be whiter than snow. Make me hear joy and happiness. . . . Make a clean heart in me, O God.

PSALM 51:1, 4, 7–8, 10 NLV

Lord, I have hurt someone. I have injured another person. And I'm filled with remorse. For not only have I harmed another, but I have disobeyed You in the process. Thus I have sinned against You at the same time. Both sins bring me shame, Lord. But doing wrong to You truly hurts my heart. So I come to You upon my knees. I ask You for forgiveness. For cleansing. For a new heart and a fresh start. Wash me within and without, Lord. Supply me with the words of apology to the person I have harmed. At the same time, Lord, help me forgive those who have hurt me. And before I leave this prayer, this place, this space, Lord, "make me hear joy and happiness" in You once more. Amen.

Grand Openings

They said to Him, "Stay with us. . . ." As [Jesus]
sat at the table with them, He took the bread and
gave thanks and broke it. Then He gave it to them.
And their eyes were opened and they knew Him.
Then He left them and could not be seen. They
said to each other, "Were not our hearts filled
with joy when He talked to us on the road
about what the Holy Writings said?"
LUKE 24:29–32 NLV

As I walk upon the road of life, Lord, thinking
about what I've seen and heard, walk with me.
Stay with me. Reveal to me the meaning of Your
Word. Open up my mind as I read Your scriptures.
Open my eyes so that I can see You in all things, all
events, from Genesis to Revelation and beyond.
Feed me the bread of Your Word. Break it open
for me so that its wisdom can pour out. Talk to me
through every letter, line, verse, and chapter. Fill
my heart with the joy of Your Word as we walk
and talk on this road and beyond. In Your name,
I pray, live, move, and have my being, amen.

Night Hours

*My lips will praise You because Your
loving-kindness is better than life. . . . On my
bed I remember You. I think of You through the
hours of the night. For You have been my help.
And I sing for joy in the shadow of Your wings.
My soul holds on to You. Your right hand holds me
up. . . . All who are faithful to God will be full of joy.*

PSALM 63:3, 6–8, 11 NLV

❧

Lord, there is no better or greater thing in my life than Your love for me and Your never-ending kindness to me. When I climb into bed at the end of the day, I think of You. I pray to You. I ask You for blessings, for compassion on me and those I love. And amid that nightly prayer to You, I not only fall asleep but fall into Your arms. Thank You for holding me, helping me, hiding me, and hovering over me. In You I find my rest, my shelter, my peace. I'm clinging to You, Lord, holding on tight. For You are my salvation. You are my joy. In You alone do I trust and find my way. Amen.

Wonder and Joy

"Why are you troubled, and why do doubts arise in your hearts? See my hands and my feet, that it is I myself. Touch me, and see. For a spirit does not have flesh and bones as you see that I have." And when he had said this, he showed them his hands and his feet. And while they still disbelieved for joy and were marveling, he said to them, "Have you anything here to eat?"

LUKE 24:38–41 ESV

You amaze me, Lord. You show up, out of nowhere, whenever I need You. You tell me to calm down. Not to worry. Not to allow thoughts of doubt into my heart or mind. You point me to You, revealing all that You are and ever have been. You tell me the truth. That You are the Son of God, the One who died to save my soul. The One raised from the dead who lives to bring me to Father God. Some days, Lord, I cannot believe what You have done for me. I sit back amazed yet full of joy. Then You help me get on with the needs of the day, continually providing for me, leading me, guiding me. Oh Lord, You are my wonder and joy. Amen.

A Willing Spirit

*Make a clean heart in me, O God. Give me a
new spirit that will not be moved. Do not throw
me away from where You are. And do not take
Your Holy Spirit from me. Let the joy of Your
saving power return to me. And give me a willing
spirit to obey you. . . . Then my tongue will sing
with joy about how right and good You are.*

PSALM 51:10–12, 14 NLV

I've fallen short, Lord. I've misstepped. And so
here I am before You, asking for forgiveness.
For my sins to be washed away. For a clean
heart—and a new spirit. One that will be stronger, not so easily led into sin, not so easily lured
into temptation. Draw me near to You, Lord. I
want to snuggle up close, to feel Your breath, to
join my spirit with Yours. Return to me the joy
of Your saving power. And make my spirit will-
ingly obey You. For I know my true joy and path
lie in Your way, not my own. Set me straight,
Lord. Prepare me and my path as I joyfully praise
You. Amen.

Open to Understanding

*He went on to open their understanding of the
Word of God, showing them how to read their
Bibles. . . . He then led them out of the city
over to Bethany. Raising his hands he blessed
them, and while blessing them, took his leave,
being carried up to heaven. And they were on
their knees, worshiping him. They returned to
Jerusalem bursting with joy. They spent all
their time in the Temple praising God.*

LUKE 24:45, 50–52 MSG

I need Your help, Lord. I need You to open my
mind, heart, and eyes as I read the Word. I want to
understand what You're writing, saying, teaching.
I want to love what You want me to love. I want
to see the words You want me to see. I want to
think the thoughts You want me to think. So lead
me, Lord. Bless me as I lift my hands in praise
and fall on my knees in worship. Give me such
a good understanding of You and Your ways that
I may return to and approach this earthly world
bursting with joy as I praise and pray in Your
name. Amen.

The Bountiful Earth

*You visit the earth and water it; you greatly
enrich it; the river of God is full of water;
you provide their grain. . . . You water its
furrows abundantly, settling its ridges,
softening it with showers, and blessing its growth.
You crown the year with your bounty. . . .
The pastures of the wilderness overflow, the hills
gird themselves with joy, the meadows clothe
themselves with flocks, the valleys deck themselves
with grain, they shout and sing together for joy.*
PSALM 65:9–13 ESV

❧

I thank You, Lord, for the gift of this earth. For
Your tender care of it and Your never-ending love
for it. Give me that same love of the earth, Lord.
Help me to be a better caretaker, to do what You
would have me do to keep its waters flowing; its
animals bountiful; its hills, plains, and meadows
alive, joyful, and productive. You are not just the
God of creation but also the Lord of abundance.
As You provide for the earth, the earth, in turn,
provides for me and mine. Help me to remember
that, Lord. To thank You for this good earth that
sings joyfully together with me in praise of You.
Amen.

Genuine Joy

Unlike the culture around you, always dragging you down to its level of immaturity, God brings the best out of you, develops well-formed maturity in you. . . . If you're called to give aid to people in distress, keep your eyes open and be quick to respond; if you work with the disadvantaged, don't let yourself get irritated with them or depressed by them. Keep a smile on your face. Love from the center of who you are; don't fake it.

ROMANS 12:2, 8–9 MSG

Help me, Lord Jesus, to be different from the culture around me. Lift me up to You, lest I be dragged down into the chaos of this world. Bring out the best in me so that I can be a useful part of Your body. Open my eyes to people whom You want me to help. Give me the resources to lift them as You have lifted me. Keep me from getting irritated by those who are weak, suffering, disadvantaged, poor, or depressed. Help me to keep my mind, heart, and ears open. Make me a good listener, free of judgment. And above all, give me such deep joy that no matter who I am helping, my smile toward them is genuine, an offshoot of my happiness in and with You. Amen.

Present Joy

[The once-exiled and now returned Israelites]
sang, praising and giving thanks to the Lord,
saying, "For He is good, for His loving-kindness
is upon Israel forever." All the people called out
with a loud voice when they praised the Lord
because the work on the house of the Lord had
begun. But many. . .had seen the first house of
the Lord. And they cried with a loud voice. . . .
But many called out for joy in a loud voice.
EZRA 3:11–12 NLV

❧

Sometimes, Lord, I can really mess up a good thing. Then when I try to rebuild, the new doesn't seem like it will be better than—or even as good as—what was there before. In either case, Lord, help me to have hope. To rejoice at whatever new thing You are doing. Although it may be okay to spend a little time grieving over the loss of what once was, don't let me stay there. Give me the courage to look away from the past and into the present. Help me to praise what You are doing now. To see the new thing You have prepared. To remember how good You have been, are now, and always will be. Enwrap me in Your present joy. In Jesus' name, amen.

The True Source

*"You heard the words that I said, 'I am not
the Christ, but I have been sent before Him.'
The man who has just been married has the bride.
The friend of the man just married stands at his
side and listens to him. He has joy when he hears
the voice of the man just married. I am full of
this joy. He must become more important.
I must become less important."*

JOHN 3:28–30 NLV

❧

Jesus, nothing gives me more joy than when I
bring You to the attention of a nonbeliever—
and then that nonbeliever begins to experience
You, follow You, love and worship You as I do.
But afterward, Lord, help me to slip away to the
sidelines. To get out of the way of Your light.
Help me to be humble enough to let the newly
born in You know *You* are the source of our joy.
That You are the true path, the real Way, and
I am just a signpost along the road. For You
alone are the one and only Son. The One who
plants and nourishes the joy in our lives and love
in our hearts. In Your name, I pray, amen.

Voices Raised in Praise

*Raise the voice of joy to God. . . . Come and see
what God has done. . . . He changed the sea into
dry land. They passed through the river on foot.
There we were full of joy in Him. . . . We went
through fire and through water. But You brought
us out into a place where we have much more
than we need. . . . Honor and thanks be to God!*
PSALM 66:1, 5–6, 12, 20 NLV

I may sometimes go through some rough patches,
Lord, but somehow You always get me out. You
make a way where there seems to be no way. You
do the impossible when I'm between a rock and
a hard place. You rescue me in a way that is so
far beyond what I ever could have dreamed or
imagined. And somehow in the process, I end
up better off than I was before! So I'm raising
my voice of joy to You, Lord. Thank You for all
You have done and continue to do in my life. All
my love, honor, and thanks go to You. In Jesus'
name, I praise, amen.

Happy in Hope

Hold on to whatever is good. Love each other. . . .
Show respect for each other. . . . Work for the Lord
with a heart full of love for Him. Be happy in your
hope. Do not give up when trouble comes. Do not
let anything stop you from praying. Share what you
have with Christian brothers who are in need. Give
meals and a place to stay to those who need it.
ROMANS 12:9–13 NLV

❧

Lord, I want to become the woman You designed
me to be. One of the spirit and not the flesh. So
I'm going to focus on all things good. I'm going
to love and respect whomever I meet. I'm going
to work for You with all my heart. And I'll be
ecstatically happy because I have hope—in You,
Your kingdom, Your promises, Your precepts, and
Your Word. Such hope will keep me joyful and
spiritually alive—even in the midst of trouble. For
I'll know You are with me—now and forever. And
as I walk Your way, I'll find myself just where You
want me: happily serving those in need, knowing
that as I do so, I'm really serving You. In Jesus'
name, amen.

Open Wide

Sing aloud to God our Strength! Shout for
joy. . . . You called in distress and I delivered you;
I answered you in the secret place of thunder;
I tested you at the waters of Meribah. . . . I am
the Lord your God, Who brought you up out of
the land of Egypt. Open your mouth wide and I
will fill it. . . . Oh, that My people would listen
to Me, that Israel would walk in My ways!
PSALM 81:1, 7, 10, 13 AMPC

From You, Lord, I get the strength to overcome.
To You, I shout for joy. Because whenever I
call, Lord, You answer. When I am in need, You
respond. You are the One who continually res-
cues me. You part the sea so I can flee from my
foes. You subdue rulers so I can find my way to
freedom in You. When I am hungry, You fill my
mouth with food. When I am thirsty, You provide
water from a rock. My joy lies in following You,
obeying You, listening to You. For only when I
walk in Your way am I on the right road, to joy
and to Your kingdom. Amen.

A Special Place

*Do not let your hearts be troubled (distressed,
agitated). You believe in and adhere to and trust
in and rely on God; believe in and adhere to
and trust in and rely also on Me. In My Father's
house there are many dwelling places (homes).
If it were not so, I would have told you; for I am
going away to prepare a place for you. . . .
Where I am going, you know the way.*

JOHN 14:1–2, 4 AMPC

꙳

Some days the woes, worries, and what-ifs come
tumbling upon me, Lord. I get weighted down by
this world so easily. And then I remember Your
words. You've told me not to let my heart and
mind be troubled but to trust in You, to lean on
and rely on God. You've made it clear that You
have a place for me in Father God's house. A
room that You have prepared—just for me! I know
the way there, so I'm running to You, Lord. Lift
me up to that room, the one where I'll find You.
That secret place of joy, where all my troubles
fade away as I melt into You. Amen.

From Sorrow to Solution

The king said to me, Why do you look sad. . . ?
This is nothing but sorrow of heart. Then I was
very much afraid. . . . The king said to me,
For what do you ask? So I prayed to the God of
heaven. And I said to [him]. . .I ask that you will
send me to Judah. . . . And the king granted what I
asked, for the good hand of my God was upon me.
NEHEMIAH 2:2, 4–5, 8 AMPC

When I am sad, Lord, when my heart is filled with sorrow, give me courage and allay my fears. Give me the words to speak to You so that I can get out from under my cloud of emotions and into the light of Your truth. Prompt me to pray, to lay out my concerns and worries before You. Help me seek Your will. Whether my prayer be long or short, spoken or silent, hear my words. Tell me what You would have me say or do. Show me which direction to go. For in You alone do I find the path to take, the courage and joy to go forward, walking with Your good hand upon me. Amen.

Never Alone

"The Father. . .will give you another Helper,
to be with you forever. . . . I will not leave you
as orphans; I will come to you. . . . If anyone
loves me, he will keep my word, and my Father
will love him, and we will come to him and
make our home with him. . . . Peace I leave with
you. . . . Let not your hearts be troubled."
JOHN 14:16, 18, 23, 27 ESV

There are times, Jesus, when I feel all alone.
When it seems as if everyone has deserted me. I
reach out, but no one is there—except for You.
Thank You for promising never to leave me. For
coming when I call You. For providing me with
Your Spirit, the Helper who takes my moans
and groans and translates them into a prayer
for God's ear. Because I love You and keep Your
Word, You and the Spirit have made a home
within me. What peace I find in You. What joy
it gives my heart to know You will always be
here with me. In Your name, I pray and praise,
amen.

How Beautiful

How beautiful are the places where You live,
O Lord of all! My soul wants and even becomes
weak from wanting to be in the house of the Lord.
My heart and my flesh sing for joy to the living
God. Even the bird has found a home. The
swallow has found a nest for herself where she
may lay her young at Your altars, O Lord
of all, my King and my God.
PSALM 84:1–3 NLV

❧

Where You live, Lord, must be amazing. I cannot even wrap my mind around what it might look like. Greater than the Taj Mahal. More amazing than the Grand Canyon. More beautiful than a Caribbean island. Wherever You are, in heaven or on earth, my soul longs to meet You, to be with You. There's no place I desire to be more than where You are. For You accept the humblest and simplest of creatures. When I, Your daughter, come to You, I feel like a princess in a palace. For in You, my Father and King, is where I find my real home. Where love, warmth, joy, and wonder rise up to greet me. As I follow Your light, I enter in, oh Lord, and bow at Your throne. Amen.

Joy Running Over

I am the Vine and you are the branches. Get your life from Me. Then I will live in you and you will give much fruit. You can do nothing without Me. . . . If you get your life from Me and My Words live in you, ask whatever you want. It will be done for you. . . . I have told you these things so My joy may be in you and your joy may be full.

JOHN 15:5, 7, 11 NLV

✧

You, Jesus, are so precious. It's in You that I find my source of love, light, and life. For I can do nothing—and *am* nothing—without You. You feed me, nourish me, and give me the power to follow Your commandments. To love the Father with all my heart, mind, soul, and strength. And to love others as I love myself. Help me, Lord, to live my life *in* You, to obey Your teachings. For when I do, You will not only live in *me* but will grant me whatever I ask. Thank You for the joy this brings—Yours in me, and mine running over! In Your name, I pray, amen.

Peace-Filled Living

Pray and give thanks for those who make
trouble for you. Yes, pray for them instead of
talking against them. Be happy with those who
are happy. Be sad with those who are sad. Live
in peace with each other. Do not act or think
with pride. Be happy to be with poor people.
Keep yourself from thinking you are so wise. . . .
As much as you can, live in peace with all men.
ROMANS 12:14–16, 18 NLV

༈

The people of this world have become so contentious, Lord. It seems to be a battleground of
continuous disagreements. And I know this is
not Your way, for spiteful comebacks suck the joy
and peace right out of life. Lord, I want to take
the higher road. So give me the words to pray for
those who make trouble for me. Help me not to
say anything bad against them but to thank You
for bringing them into my life. Help me to treat
others with compassion and to be the peacemaker
in all situations. In other words, Lord Jesus, give
me the strength, courage, and fortitude to be more
like You—acquainted with sorrow yet, in praying
and serving others, transformed by joy. In Your
name, I pray, amen.

Gentle Strength

How happy are those who live in Your house!
They are always giving thanks to You. How
happy is the man whose strength is in You and in
whose heart are the roads to Zion! As they pass
through the dry valley of Baca, they make it a place
of good water. The early rain fills the pools with
good also. They go from strength to strength.
Every one of them stands before God.
PSALM 84:4–7 NLV

The more time I spend with You, Jesus—studying Your Word, praying Your way, absorbing Your truths, following Your will—the stronger I seem to become. At each point, in each trial, I learn more, grow more, and find myself closer and closer to You. Yet at the same time my strength is increasing, the gentler I become and the more I find peace, even in the midst of trial. All this gives me such joy. The unshakable kind. The joy that makes my foundation in You so firm. Thank You, Lord, for being there—everywhere I look. Everywhere I love. Everywhere I roam, from strength to strength, I'm home in You. Amen.

Birthing Joy

When a woman gives birth, she has a hard time,
there's no getting around it. But when the baby
is born, there is joy in the birth. This new life
in the world wipes out memory of the pain. The
sadness you have right now is similar to that pain,
but the coming joy is also similar. When I see
you again, you'll be full of joy, and it will
be a joy no one can rob from you.
JOHN 16:21–23 MSG

It's so true, Lord! When a woman is pregnant, she
and her body go through a lot. First she's happy
she's going to have a baby. Then she may have
morning sickness, become physically awkward,
and have to get up several times at night to re-
lieve herself. And that's just the prelude to the
overture of pain that comes with giving birth.
Yet when she holds that baby, that gift of life in
her arms, the love she has for that child erases
all the prior pain. And it's the same with lots of
other things in life, Lord. I may have hard times,
but because You're with me through the trials, I
know I'll find the joy I desire in You, from pain
to pleasure, from beginning to end. Amen.

Happy in Jesus

O Lord God of all, hear my prayer. . . .
Look upon our safe-covering, O God. And look
upon the face of Your chosen one. For a day in
Your house is better than a thousand outside. . . .
For the Lord God is a sun and a safe-covering. . . .
He holds back nothing good from those who
walk in the way that is right. O Lord of all,
how happy is the man who trusts in You!
PSALM 84:8–12 NLV

❧

After a week in the world, Lord, I run to Your house of worship. I run to join Your other children in prayer and praise as we lift our eyes and hearts to You. Thank You, Lord, for keeping me safe, looking out for me from Monday to Saturday. Thank You for coming into our presence when we come to Your house. Every minute there is so precious. For I see Your love and light in those who worship with me, Lord. We happily trust You, Lord, to help us, to meet with us, to keep us strong as we endeavor to serve You. Amen.

Completed with Joy

Forget about deciding what's right for each other. . . . God's kingdom isn't a matter of what you put in your stomach, for goodness' sake. It's what God does with your life as he sets it right, puts it together, and completes it with joy. Your task is to single-mindedly serve Christ. Do that and you'll kill two birds with one stone: pleasing the God above you and proving your worth to the people around you.

ROMANS 14:13, 17–18 MSG

Jesus, there are so many traditions, rules, and methods people say should be used to serve You, love You, pray to You, worship You, and more. It's mind-boggling. All I want is to follow what You would have me do. So help me to focus on You more than any other thing. Help me to dive deeply into Your Word for direction. To concentrate on serving You and You alone. For I know when I do, the Father will use me as He desires and fill my life with joy. What more can a woman ask but to please Father God and be of worth to those around her? In Jesus' name, amen.

Lord Knows

The heart knows its own bitterness, and no stranger shares its joy. . . . In the reverent and worshipful fear of the Lord there is strong confidence, and His children shall always have a place of refuge. . . . A calm and undisturbed mind and heart are the life and health of the body. . . . Wisdom rests [silently] in the mind and heart of him who has understanding.

PROVERBS 14:10, 26, 30, 33 AMPC

Only You can fully understand and empathize with the sorrow I bear in my heart, Lord. And yet at the same time, only You can fully understand, know, and take part in the joy I experience as well. Whether joyful or sad, I know You are with me, tending me, caring for me, crying or laughing with me. In You I find shelter from the storms of life. You give me the peace I crave. You calm my heart, quiet my spirit. Give me the wisdom, Lord, to run to You whether I am in tears or rolling with laughter. Share my life, sorrows, and joys, Lord, as I live and move in You. Amen.

From Sadness to Gladness

You're going to be in deep mourning while the godless world throws a party. You'll be sad, very sad, but your sadness will develop into gladness. . . . This is what I want you to do: Ask the Father for whatever is in keeping with the things I've revealed to you. Ask in my name, according to my will, and he'll most certainly give it to you. Your joy will be a river overflowing its banks!

JOHN 16:20, 23–24 MSG

❦

I'm looking to You for direction, Jesus. I want to walk in Your way, according to Your will. You are the way and truth and life. While You were here on earth and now while You're in heaven, You know exactly what's going to happen in my life and why. You have said my path lies in You. Show me, Jesus, what You would have me pray for, what You would have me ask for. Align my heart, mind, and desires so they are in line with Yours. For I know that as You do so, my "sadness will develop into gladness." My joy will overflow its banks. In Your precious name, I pray, amen.

Joy-Giver

*Lord God of all, powerful Lord, who is like
You? All around You we see how faithful
You are. You rule over the rising sea. When
its waves rise, You quiet them. . . . You have
a strong arm. Your hand is powerful. . . .
Your throne stands on what is right and fair.
Loving-kindness and truth go before You. How
happy are the people who know the sound of joy!*
PSALM 89:8–9, 13–15 NLV

I'm amazed, Lord, at how faithful You are to
me. Especially when I have erred, slipped up, or
been unfaithful to You. Thank You, God, that You
are in control of not just *my* life but everyone's
life, as well as this world's ebb and flow. That
gives me hope, Lord. And hope opens the door to
joy—not just for me but for everyone, everything,
all that You have created. Nothing can over-
power You, Lord. So I'm clinging to You. I'm
waiting for You, Your justice, Your peace, Your
favor, Your strength, Your saving grace. And as
I wait, I'm going to trust in You, my Joy-Giver.
For in You is goodness. In You is calm. In You,
I'm sound and saved. Amen.

The Morning Star Rises

*We have the prophetic word. . . . You will do well
to pay close attention to it as to a lamp shining in
a dismal (squalid and dark) place, until the day
breaks through [the gloom] and the Morning Star
rises (comes into being) in your hearts. . . . I
waited patiently and expectantly for the Lord. . . .
[She proudly said] I am my beloved's, and his
desire is toward me! . . . Come, my beloved!*

2 Peter 1:19; Psalm 40:1;
Song of Solomon 7:10–11 AMPC

❧

Be with me, Lord Jesus, as I enter Your Word.
Help me not just to read it but to take it in,
absorb it, and allow it to work its way into my
life. Let the light and power of Your Word break
through the gloom within me until You rise up
and come into being within my heart, changing whatever sorrows that linger into joy. You are
my bright Morning Star, Jesus. For You I patiently
wait. It is Your presence I expect to change me
from the inside out, letter by letter, word by
word. You are my Beloved. Desire me as I desire
You. Come, Jesus; come now. Amen.

Walking on Air

*Blessed are the people who know the passwords
of praise, who shout on parade in the bright
presence of GOD. Delighted, they dance all day
long; they know who you are, what you do—
they can't keep it quiet! Your vibrant beauty has
gotten inside us—you've been so good to us!
We're walking on air! All we are and have we
owe to GOD, Holy God of Israel, our King!*

PSALM 89:15–18 MSG

At times, Lord, I can't see the forest for the trees;
I can't see the good within the bad. Although
that seems the natural way of humankind, I know
that's not how You want us to view the world.
For when we see only the perils and darkness,
we miss the safety and light. So help change me
up, Lord. Help me focus more on the showers
of blessings, the good, the light. Prompt me to
dance and shout in praise. Remind me of who
You are, what You've done. Fill me with such
joy and delight that I'm lifted way above the
earth, praising You all the day. In Jesus' name,
I pray, amen.

Joy-Makers

We who are strong [in our convictions and of robust faith] ought to bear with the failings and the frailties and the tender scruples of the weak; [we ought to help carry the doubts and qualms of others] and not to please ourselves. Let each one of us make it a practice to please (make happy) his neighbor for his good and for his true welfare, to edify him [to strengthen him and build him up spiritually].

ROMANS 15:1–2 AMPC

Lord, I feel so blessed to be aware of the role that joy plays in my life. But this joy is not just for me alone. This joy is something I can use to help others. So each day, Lord, as I hope in You, count my blessings, and revel in the joy of You, remind me to help others, those who are not as strong in their faith. Help me to please You by helping to please them, to make them happy, to bring a smile to their faces, to encourage them, to build them up in their spirits. In other words, Lord, use me to spread Your joy, from here to eternity! In Jesus' name, I pray, amen.

True Happiness

*Then Haman went out that day glad and with joy
in his heart. But when he saw Mordecai at the
king's gate, and when he did not stand up or show
any fear in front of him, Haman was filled with
anger. . . . For the Jews it was a time of joy and
happiness and honor. In every part of the nation
and in every city where the king's law had come,
there was happiness and joy for the Jews.*
ESTHER 5:9; 8:16–17 NLV

It's interesting, Lord, how I need to be sure of
my source of joy. Does the joy I find in my life
come from the deep well of knowing You, seeking
You, and abiding in You? Or does my joy come
from the shallow stream that eddies around my
self-pride, honor, and worldly ambitions? The
test seems to be that if my joy comes from the
deep well of pleasing You instead of the shallow
stream of pleasing myself and the world, my happiness will not be fleeting but a deep, constant,
and abiding joy. Help me seek my joy and happiness in You alone, Lord. For then I will find
the everlasting gladness that comes only by living for and in You. Amen.

Joy in the Journey

*Everything that was written in the Holy
Writings long ago was written to teach us.
By not giving up, God's Word gives us strength
and hope. Now the God Who helps you not to
give up and gives you strength will help you think
so you can please each other as Christ Jesus did.
Then all of you together can thank the God
and Father of our Lord Jesus Christ.*
ROMANS 15:4–6 NLV

❧

Thank You, Lord, for the Old Testament writings
that teach me about You, Your Son, Your Spirit—
and myself. The stories that teach me so many
valuable lessons, including the one about Joseph.
So many things were against him, Lord. Yet even
though he'd been sold into servitude, unjustly
accused, and then jailed, Joseph continued to be
positive, hopeful, and joyful—and so prospered.
For he knew You were with him *and* that although
others had planned evil against him, You would
use those same plans for his good (see Genesis
50:20)! Help me, Lord, to have that same trust
that You're with me, that same assurance that all
that happens—including the seemingly bad—will
work out for my good. For then I too will find
joy and success in my journey with You. Amen.

Safety, Security, and Guidance

The Lord. . .heard my cry. He drew me up out
of a horrible pit [a pit of tumult and of destruction],
out of the miry clay (froth and slime), and set
my feet upon a rock, steadying my steps and
establishing my goings. And He has put a new song
in my mouth, a song of praise to our God. . . .
Blessed (happy, fortunate, to be envied) is the
man who makes the Lord his refuge and trust.
PSALM 40:1–4 AMPC

Oh Lord my God, You make my heart sing. For
when I'm in trouble and call out to You, You respond immediately. You pull me out of peril, set
my feet firmly on a rock, then steady my steps.
You bless me with safety, security, and guidance.
And then, on top of all that, You put a new song
in my mouth so that I cannot help but praise You
from here to kingdom come! I truly am happy,
overflowing with joy, because I have You, Lord.
Because I have made You my shelter, my refuge
from life's storms. In You, I put all my trust. Thank
You, Lord, for all these blessings and more. Amen.

Joy in the Challenge

*Peter answered Him, Lord, if it is You, command
me to come to You on the water. He said, Come!
So Peter got out of the boat and walked on the
water, and he came toward Jesus. But when
he perceived and felt the strong wind, he was
frightened, and as he began to sink, he cried
out, Lord, save me [from death]! Instantly Jesus
reached out His hand and caught and held him.*
MATTHEW 14:28–31 AMPC

～♪♪～

You, Jesus, have a way of taking Your followers
out of their comfort zones. First, You direct Your
disciples to cross the sea. The next thing they
know, they're desperately trying to ride out a
storm. Yet before they even cry out for help, You
appear in a miraculous way, walking on the water.
You yell over their screams, telling them to be
brave. Peter then takes another challenge and
begins to walk toward You. But seeing the wind
and waves, he cries out to You—and immediately
You grab hold of him. You, Lord, are the joy I
find in all my challenges. With my eyes on You,
I can do all things, knowing You'll be ready to
catch me. Amen.

From Hope to Joy and Peace

Isaiah says, "There will be One from the family of Jesse Who will be a leader over the people who are not Jews. Their hope will be in Him." Our hope comes from God. May He fill you with joy and peace because of your trust in Him. May your hope grow stronger by the power of the Holy Spirit. . . . May our God Who gives us peace, be with you all. Let it be so.
ROMANS 15:12–13, 33 NLV

❧

My hope is bound up in You, Jesus. For You are the One I look to, the One I live for because You lead me through sun and shade. You build me up, strengthen me, encourage me, renew and refresh me. I trust You to get me through every wilderness wandering. And because of my hope and trust in You, God fills me with the joy and peace so lacking in this world. Help me, Lord, to lay myself open to You and Your way. To follow the leadings of the Spirit, to allow Him to have greater sway over my life, so that I will be stronger and better able to serve You with peace of mind and heart. Lord, let it be so, amen.

Constant Conversation

*Many, O Lord my God, are the wonderful works
which You have done, and Your thoughts toward
us; no one can compare with You! If I should
declare and speak of them, they are too many to
be numbered. . . . I delight to do Your will, O my
God; yes, Your law is within my heart. . . . Let
all those that seek and require You rejoice and be
glad in You. . .my Help and my Deliverer.*
PSALM 40:5, 8, 16–17 AMPC

I don't just want You, Lord, but I seek You out,
wherever I am, whatever I'm doing. I'm in constant conversation with You because I need You
more than anything else in this world and the
next. There is no greater Guide than You. No
greater Power, Force, Refuge, Strengthener. You
don't just help me, Lord; You deliver me. You get
me out of so many sticky situations, often ones
that I myself have made. Make me ever more
aware of Your presence and my need for You,
Lord. In You I find all the joy I could ever hope
for or imagine. In Jesus' name, amen.

Forever Prayer

"While I have been with [My followers] in the world, I have kept them in the power of Your name. I have kept watch over those You gave Me . . . . But now I come to You, Father. I say these things while I am in the world. In this way, My followers may have My joy in their hearts. . . . I do not pray for these followers only. I pray for those who will put their trust in Me."

JOHN 17:12–13, 20 NLV

At times, Jesus, I don't feel very loved or even lovable. I feel unprotected, alone. And then, with all the strength I can muster, I turn to You. I open Your Word. And there I find the comfort, love, safety, and joy I long for. For You, Lord, are watching over me. You keep me safe in the power of God's name. And before You gave up Your life for mine, You even *prayed* to God for *me*! I am one who lives with her trust in You. And this prayer You prayed for me is still rising up with the smoke of incense in the presence of God from the hand of the angel (see Revelation 8:4). I'm overwhelmed, Lord, with joy from and in You, my forever Prayer. Amen.

Protecting Angels

He who dwells in the secret place of the Most
High shall remain stable and fixed under the
shadow of the Almighty [Whose power no foe
can withstand]. I will say of the Lord, He is my
Refuge and my Fortress, my God; on Him I lean
and rely, and in Him I [confidently] trust! . . . He
will cover you. . . . You shall not be afraid. . . .
He will give His angels [especial] charge over you.
PSALM 91:1–2, 4–5, 11 AMPC

When I'm not trusting You, Lord, worry and
dread take all the joy out of my life. So when
I'm in that dark place of fretting and fearing, lift
me up to that secret place—Your presence. Only
there will I find the safety and courage I need!
For when I'm in that place, nothing—within or
without—can withstand Your power. Lord, my
Refuge and Fortress, on You alone I'm leaning
and relying. In You I'm putting all my trust. In
You alone do I gain the strength and courage I
need to face the day and find the joy that comes
from knowing Your angels are watching over me.
So be it—amen!

Encamped in Hope

I saw the Lord constantly before me, for He is at my right hand that I may not be shaken or overthrown or cast down [from my secure and happy state]. Therefore my heart rejoiced and my tongue exulted exceedingly; moreover, my flesh also will dwell in hope [will encamp, pitch its tent, and dwell in hope]. . . . You have made known to me the ways of life; You will enrapture me [diffusing my soul with joy] with and in Your presence.
ACTS 2:25–26, 28 AMPC

❧

Lord Jesus, I want You constantly before me, beside me, within me. I want to see this world through Your eyes. In that way, I will never be shaken, brought low, or struck with a worldly mind-set. With You in and with me, I will stay safe and secure. I will find all the joy I can handle. I'm driving stakes into the ground of hope. There my tent will be pitched, stable, unmovable. There is where I will live this life—happy in Your presence, where You'll fill my spirit and spread Your joy upon my soul. In Your love, Your strength, Your presence, and Your name, I pray, amen.

A Story to Glory

*What a beautiful thing, GOD, to give thanks,
to sing an anthem to you, the High God! To
announce your love each daybreak, sing your
faithful presence all through the night. . . . You
made me so happy, GOD. I saw your work and
I shouted for joy. . . . My ears are filled with
the sounds of promise: "Good people will prosper.
. . . They'll grow tall in the presence of God,
lithe and green, virile still in old age."*

PSALM 92:1–2, 4, 11–14 MSG

When the world tries to drag me down into hopelessness, I'm going to fight back. I'm going to give thanks to You, Lord. I'm going to sing Your praises, proclaim how much You love me. I'm going to keep You with me throughout the day and then sing about how faithful You are to me at night. All my joy and happiness are bound up in Your promises and presence. As I look around me and see all the wonders You have created, I'll shout for joy. I'll revel in wonder. I'll grow tall in Your garden and continue to be productive even when I'm old. May I be a story reflecting Your glory. In Jesus' name, amen.

Rejoicing on the Way

An angel of the Lord said to Philip,
"Rise and go.". . . And he rose and went. . . .
The Spirit said to Philip, "Go over and join
this chariot." So Philip ran to [the eunuch]. . . .
And [Philip] baptized him. And when they came
up out of the water, the Spirit of the Lord carried
Philip away, and the eunuch saw him no more,
and went on his way rejoicing.
ACTS 8:26–27, 29–30, 38–39 ESV

Lord, I love living in Your Word, experiencing Your joy, growing in my faith. But You want me to do more. You want me to share You with others so that they too can experience all those things, all those blessings in, with, and from You. So today, Lord, I pray that You would keep me ever attentive to Your direction. That You would open my ears to the voice of Your Spirit. And that once I hear that voice, You would enable me to go where the Spirit wants me to go, do what He wants me to do, and say what He wants me to say so that others can go on Your way rejoicing. In Jesus' name, I pray, amen.

Small Beginning, Greater End

If you will seek God diligently and make your supplication to the Almighty, then, if you are pure and upright, surely He will bestir Himself for you and make your righteous dwelling prosperous again. And though your beginning was small, yet your latter end would greatly increase. . . . Behold, as surely as God will never uphold wrongdoers, He will never cast away a blameless man. He will yet fill your mouth with laughter. . .and your lips with joyful shouting.

JOB 8:5–7, 20–21 AMPC

When things seem to be going badly, when nothing seems to be going my way, Lord, I hang on to the hope that You will hear and answer my prayer. For Your Son has made me pure and blameless in Your eyes. Your Son has paved the way so that when I seek after You and lift my soul to You, You bend Your ear to my lips. I believe, Lord, that You will not only move on my behalf but make things better than they were before—in Your own time. I believe, Lord, that You will never turn away but will erase my tears. You, in Your love and compassion, will once again fill my mouth with laughter and my lips with shouts of joy. In Jesus' name, I pray, amen.

The Right Way to Joy

*To do what is right and good and fair is more
pleasing to the Lord than gifts given on the altar
in worship. . . . When what is right and fair
is done, it is a joy for those who are right with
God. . . . He who follows what is right and loving
and kind finds life, right-standing with God and
honor. . . . The horse is made ready for war,
but winning the fight belongs to the Lord.*

PROVERBS 21:3, 15, 21, 31 NLV

Lord, sometimes I just don't understand this
world. So many people think they hold the right
answers, yet those answers are not of You. They
don't jive with what You would have Your followers be and do. Yet the "right people" who
appear to be "wrong in You" seem to be increasing. Justice seems to be the golden ring society
rarely obtains. So I'm looking to You, Lord. Help
me do what is right, good, and fair in Your eyes.
Give me the strength to please You alone, despite
the people pleasers who surround me. Help me
follow the good way, the right path, *Your* path,
leaving the results to You. For only then will I
find joy the "right" way. Amen.

Freedom in Joy

*Peter was held in prison. But the church kept
praying to God for him. . . . Peter was sleeping
between two soldiers. . . . The angel hit Peter on
the side and said, "Get up!" Then the chains
fell off his hands. . . . He went to Mary's house
. . . . Peter knocked at the gate. . . . In her joy
[Rhoda] forgot to open the gate. She ran in and
told them that Peter was standing outside.*

ACTS 12:5–7, 12–14 NLV

The joy of answered prayer! The joy in knowing
we have access to You. The happiness in the
knowledge that we can come to You, give You
our heartfelt concerns, and know You have heard
us and will act on our behalf. The power You
exude in response—reaching across time and
space, sending down Your angels, and having
them work out Your will in Your way as You free
us, our family, our friends, and total strangers
from the constraints that bind us. Lord, thank
You for hearing our prayers. For moving on our
behalf. For the answers You provide, ones that
defy all expectations and imaginations, and leave
us overcome with joy. Amen.

From Dawn to Dusk

He spread a cloud for a covering, and fire to give light at night. They asked, and He brought them quails for meat. And He filled them with the bread of heaven. He opened the rock and water flowed out. It flowed in the desert like a river. For He remembered His holy Word. . . . He brought His people out with joy, His chosen ones with singing.

PSALM 105:39–43 NLV

❦

When I need to hide, Lord, You protect me, covering me with a cloud. When I am walking in darkness, in the deep shadows of night, You provide a fire to give light. When I ask for food, when I thirst for water, You provide both in abundance. You remember Your promises and You keep Your word. All the ways You take care of me are more than I can fathom, Lord. Be with me once more this day, from the time I begin my work for You until the moment I lay down my head. Bring me through, Lord, with joy. May my last thoughts be songs of praise to You. In Jesus' name, amen.

Two Things. . .

Two things I have asked of You. . . . Take lies and
what is false far from me. Do not let me be poor
or rich. Feed me with the food that I need. Then
I will not be afraid that I will be full and turn my
back against You and say, "Who is the Lord?" And
I will not be afraid that I will be poor and steal,
and bring shame on the name of my God.

PROVERBS 30:7–9 NLV

Two things that steal joy, Lord: getting caught
in a snare of lies and living in a state of discon-
tentment. So I bring You this prayer. First, Lord,
please give me the courage to be honest. For all
lies are against You, the God of truth. Second,
Lord, please grant me enough to live on—no
more, no less. Not more because I don't want
"stuff"—possessions, treasures on earth—to come
between me and You. Yet not less so that I won't
have to depend on others or be tempted to take
from others and bring disgrace to me and You.
That's it, Lord. The truth and enough to get by.
That will be all I need to gain, maintain, and proclaim my joy in You! In Jesus' name, I pray, amen.

Good Things

Some traveled through the desert wastes. They did not find a way. . . . Their souls became weak within them. Then they cried out to the Lord in their trouble. And He took them out of their suffering. He led them by a straight path. . . . He fills the thirsty soul. And He fills the hungry soul with good things. . . . Let them give Him gifts of thanks and tell of His works with songs of joy.

PSALM 107:4–7, 9, 22 NLV

So often, Lord, I find myself just wandering. I cannot find my way in, out, over, around, under, or through. And as I go on wandering, my soul grows weak within me. Then I look up. I cry to You, longing to see Your face. And You come quickly. You lift me up, turn me around, show me the right way to go. As I follow Your directions, I see glimpses of You out ahead of me, beckoning, encouraging, loving. And in the resting places, You quench my thirsty and hungering soul with good—all that I need to thrive, to continue on with You. It is for this and so much more that I sing a song of praise and joy to You, the God of my life. Amen.

Power Released

He, having received [so strict a] charge, put them into the inner prison (the dungeon) and fastened their feet in the stocks. But about midnight, as Paul and Silas were praying and singing hymns of praise to God, and the [other] prisoners were listening to them, suddenly there was a great earthquake, so that the very foundations of the prison were shaken; and at once all the doors were opened and everyone's shackles were unfastened.

ACTS 16:24–26 AMPC

❧

It's true, Lord, that sometimes joy leads me into praising You. But oftentimes, I find that even when joy seems elusive, when I just can't get there from where I am, praise pulls my heart out of the darkness and my mind off its troubles and brings me right smack into joy! So here I am, Lord, coming to You chained by my sorrow, my mood, my darkness. I'm raising my voice in praise and song to You. And as I do, as my words leave my lips and rise up to Your ears, I find Your power unleashed. The foundation of my troubles, worries, and what-ifs is shaken to its core! And all at once, my door to You, to joy, is opened. I'm free of my shackles! Thank You for releasing me and pulling me up into You! Amen!

Into His Keeping

[The jailer]. . . .fell down before Paul and Silas. . . .
Men, what is it necessary for me to do that I
may be saved? And they answered, Believe in the
Lord Jesus Christ [give yourself up to Him, take
yourself out of your own keeping and entrust
yourself into His keeping] and you will be saved,
[and this applies both to] you and your household
as well. . . . Then he. . .leaped much for joy.
ACTS 16:29–31, 34 AMPC

So often, Lord, I find that I really haven't given
You all of me. I attempt to take care of myself, to
trust my own skills, resources, and knowledge. I actually think I know better than You! Today, Jesus,
make me a woman totally in Your keeping. Help
me give You all of me, to leave nothing behind.
To entrust all things to You—my mind, body,
soul, spirit, family, friends, country, possessions,
present, and future. Remind me of Your power,
grace, forgiveness, and wisdom. Help me get it
through my head that only by taking myself out
of my own keeping and into Yours will I find the
joy that will make me want to leap, to dance, to
sing in Your name. Amen.

Word Welcomed

They answered, Believe in the Lord Jesus Christ. . . . And they declared the Word of the Lord. . . . And he took them the same hour of the night and bathed [them because of their bloody] wounds. . . . Then he took them up into his house and set food before them; and he leaped much for joy and exulted with all his family that he believed in God [accepting and joyously welcoming what He had made known through Christ].

ACTS 16:31–34 AMPC

❧

Oh gentlest of Saviors, how much You still have to teach me. I *do* believe in You. I put myself entirely in Your keeping, leaving no remainder behind to fret or fear. And then I read Your Word, and my eyes are opened. My heart moved. Your gentleness prompts me to be gentle to others—the chained, injured, and lost. To pull them close to me and to tend to their wounds. To share what I have with them. For as Your Word fills every crevice of want and desire, I am led to You, Your power, Your grace, Your love, and Your light, which then flow through me and onto others. Your Word is more than welcome in my life, Lord. It *is* my life. Amen.

Home Once More

*Some sat in darkness and in the shadow of death.
They suffered in prison in iron chains. Because
they had turned against the Words of God. . . .
Then they cried out to the Lord in their trouble.
And He saved them. . . . He brought them out
of darkness and the shadow of death. And He
broke their chains. . . . Let them give Him gifts of
thanks and tell of His works with songs of joy.*

PSALM 107:10–11, 13–14, 22 NLV

Even when I go against Your Word, Lord, You save
me. Even when my own stubbornness leads me
away from Your will and toward my own, You hear
my cry. When all around is darkness, You bring
me back out into the light of Your way. You break
the ties that have bound me. And once again I am
humbled. I can barely look up at You. For although
I am full of joy that I am back in Your light, I am
full of shame. Why am I so willful? Forgive me,
Lord. Pull me into Your compassionate embrace.
Hold me tight as I snuggle back into Your warmth,
so glad to be home with You once more. Amen.

Enjoying the Days

I know that it will be well for those who fear God.
. . . But it will not go well for the sinful. . . . There
are right and good men who have the same thing
happen to them that happens to those who do sinful
things. And there are sinful men who have the same
thing happen to them that happens to those who are
right and good. . . . So I say a man should enjoy
himself. . . . Eat and drink and be happy. . .
through the days. . .which God has given him.

ECCLESIASTES 8:12–15 NLV

❧

I keep waiting, Lord, for bad people to "get theirs."
But they never seem to! And Your Word says
that's just how it is. Sometimes bad things happen to good people, and good things happen to
bad people. At least on earth, anyway. So help
me, Lord, to turn all these thoughts over to You.
To realize I'll never be able to figure everything
out, but You have, and You will take care of it.
Meanwhile, I'm going to enjoy my days with You
right here, right now. I'm going to live and be joy
filled in Your name. Amen!

A Lode of Joy

In all our affliction, I am overflowing with joy.
For even when we came into Macedonia, our
bodies had no rest, but we were afflicted at every
turn—fighting without and fear within. But God,
who comforts the downcast, comforted us by the
coming of Titus, and not only by his coming but
also by the comfort with which he was comforted
by you. . .so that I rejoiced still more.
2 CORINTHIANS 7:4–7 ESV

It's amazing, Lord, how contagious our emotions
can be! What I express has an effect on all those
around me! So help me, Lord, to overflow with
joy—no matter what is going on in my life. To
find and tap into that deep, abiding lode of spiritual joy You have waiting for me, streaming just
beneath the surface. For as You comfort me and fill
me with gladness, my friends, family, coworkers,
and even complete strangers will find themselves
eased in their own pain and affliction. Our fighting without and fears within will dissipate and
become as nothing but fool's gold, something
that is easily thrown away as we treasure what
we have in You! Amen!

Heavenly Dew

You will guard him and keep him in perfect and constant peace whose mind [both its inclination and its character] is stayed on You, because he commits himself to You, leans on You, and hopes confidently in You. So trust in the Lord (commit yourself to Him, lean on Him, hope confidently in Him) forever. . . . You who dwell in the dust, awake and sing for joy! For Your dew [O Lord] is a dew of [sparkling] light [heavenly, supernatural dew].

ISAIAH 26:3–4, 19 AMPC

༝ཞ

I'm keeping my mind, heart, soul, and spirit focused on You, Lord. For when I do, Your guard of peace comes up all around me. Its shield keeps me still within, no matter what is happening without. In You I find my refuge, for to You alone I am committed. On You alone I lean. All my hope and expectation lie in You—not just today, in this moment on earth, but forever. Beyond this day and all the days to come. Rain down Your love upon me, Lord. For it's Your refreshment that keeps me from running dry and in the current of Your presence and all the love and joy that come with it. Amen.

Eagerly Awaiting

*I bore you on eagles' wings and brought you
to Myself. . . . The eternal God is your refuge
and dwelling place, and underneath are the
everlasting arms. . . . [Looking forward to the
shepherd's arrival, the eager girl pictures their
meeting and says]. . .Oh, that his left hand
were under my head and that his right hand
embraced me! . . . Let all those that seek and
require You rejoice and be glad in You.*
EXODUS 19:4; DEUTERONOMY 33:27;
SONG OF SOLOMON 8:1, 3; PSALM 40:16 AMPC

Lord, thank You for hovering over me. For bearing
me on eagles' wings, bringing me out of myself and
into You. You are my refuge. In You I live, move,
and have my being. You hold me up when I'm
down. You turn my life around. Each and every
morning, I look for You, eagerly anticipating the
calm, peace, love, and joy I'll experience when
Your left hand gently cradles my head and Your
right hand draws me into You. Come, Lord. I'm
waiting. I'm willing and ready to melt into Your
love and affection. In Jesus' name, I pray, amen.

A Joyful Walk with Jesus

I am going. . .bound by the [Holy] Spirit and obligated and compelled by the [convictions of my own] spirit, not knowing what will befall me. . . except that the Holy Spirit clearly and emphatically affirms to me. . .that imprisonment and suffering await me. But none of these things move me; neither do I esteem my life dear to myself, if only I may finish my course with joy and the ministry which I have obtained from [which was entrusted to me by] the Lord Jesus.

ACTS 20:22–24 AMPC

❧

I'm not really sure what lies before me, Lord. Only You can see all things that have been, are, and will be. But I know that Your Spirit is leading my spirit, urging me to move ahead, to continue on with the gifts You have given me, in the direction You have sent me. Whatever happens, good or bad, doesn't really matter to me. The only desire I have is to finish my walk with You with joy, working where and when You allow. Thank You, Lord, for making me a part of Your plan. In Jesus' name, I pray, amen.

Healing Word

Some were fools because of their wrong-doing.
They had troubles because of their sins. . . .
And they came near the gates of death. Then they
cried out to the Lord in their trouble. And He
saved them from their suffering. He sent His Word
and healed them. And He saved them from the
grave. . . . Let them give Him gifts of thanks
and tell of His works with songs of joy.
PSALM 107:17–20, 22 NLV

Whenever I miss the target You've set for me,
Lord, trouble follows. Only then, it seems, do I
stop and regret the things I said or did. Only then
do I cry out for You to save me from the conse-
quences of my sin. And even then, in those times
when I'm not proud of myself in any way, shape,
or form, You come when I call. You save me, pull
me out, lift me up, restore me. You send Your Word
to heal me. You give me life once more. There is
no way I can ever repay all You do for me, Lord.
All I can offer is my humble thanks and songs of
joy, love, and gratitude. Amen.

Open to Joy

Give strength to weak hands and to weak knees.
Say to those whose heart is afraid, "Have strength
of heart, and do not be afraid. See, your God
will come. . . . He will save you." Then the eyes
of the blind will be opened. And the ears of those
who cannot hear will be opened. Then those who
cannot walk will jump like a deer. And the tongue
of those who cannot speak will call out for joy.
ISAIAH 35:3–6 NLV

Your Word, Lord—oh, how it feeds every part of me! It gives strength, power, and energy to my weak hands and knees. Your Word swells my heart, filling it with the courage I need to face things I'd rather not face, things I can overcome only when You stand with me. Your Word opens the eyes of my heart each time I look within its pages. Your voice reveals new meanings, helping me to understand things that were once cloudy. You make me want to leap and shout for joy! Continue with me, Lord. Today reveal the wonder and power of Your Word until my soul once again rejoices. Amen.

Giving First to God

*[The Macedonian churches] have been put to
the test by much trouble, but they have much joy.
They have given much even though they were very
poor. They gave as much as they could because
they wanted to. They asked from their hearts if
they could help the Christians in Jerusalem. It was
more than we expected. They gave themselves
to the Lord first. Then they gave themselves to
us to be used as the Lord wanted.*

2 Corinthians 8:2–5 NLV

There is such joy in giving, Lord. But there are so
many worthy causes. It can be difficult to know
which to choose. So, Lord, make Your desires clear
to me. As I give myself first to You, I'm relying
on You to help me to home in on the causes You
want me to support through service, provisions,
or money. Lord, I want to give from the heart and
soul. And after I do, I'm not going to worry about
where my next dollar will be coming from but will
rely on You to provide for me as I help provide
for others—with absolute joy and pleasure. In
Jesus' name, amen.

A Joyful Comeback

"Come back to me and really mean it!" . . .
*Change your life, not just your clothes. Come back
to* GOD, *your God. And here's why: God is kind
and merciful. He takes a deep breath, puts up with
a lot, this most patient God, extravagant in love,
always ready to cancel catastrophe. Who knows?
Maybe he'll do it now, maybe he'll turn around
and show pity. Maybe, when all's said and done,
there'll be blessings full and robust for your* GOD!
JOEL 2:12–14 MSG

Lord, I know sometimes I'm just not there for You.
Not like You're always here for me. I've gotten so
busy living life, I've forgotten to live it for You! As
a result, all joy seems to have gone out of me. So
forgive me, God, for wandering away. I know You
are kind, loving, and compassionate. You have so
much more love for me than I do for myself right
now, Lord. So let's change things up. As I come
back to You, Lord, come back to me. Turn my life
around to the good. Shower Your blessings upon
me as I joyfully await Your power and presence in
my life once more! In Jesus' name, amen.

Freedom to Choose

You were chosen to be free. Be careful that you do not please your old selves by sinning because you are free. Live this free life by loving and helping others. . . . Let the Holy Spirit lead you in each step. Then you will not please your sinful old selves. . . . The fruit that comes from having the Holy Spirit in our lives is: love, joy, peace, not giving up, being kind, being good, having faith, being gentle, and being the boss over our own desires.

GALATIANS 5:13, 16, 22–23 NLV

Your Word, Lord, makes it clear that You *chose* me to be free! For that privilege I praise You, Lord. Yet I don't want that same freedom to lead me to please myself. I want to please *You*. And the only way to do that is by letting Your Holy Spirit lead me in every way, every day. So help me, Lord, to keep close to You. To home in on what the Holy Spirit would have me do, where He would have me go. Then I will have the love, joy, peace, and so much more that comes from walking in Your will and way! In Jesus' name, I pray, amen.

Regaining Strength

Let them give Him gifts of thanks and tell of His
works with songs of joy. Some went out to sea in
ships. . . . He spoke and raised up a storm. . . .
Their strength of heart left them in their danger. . . .
They did not know what to do. Then they cried out
to the Lord in their trouble. And He took them out
of all their problems. He stopped the storm, and
the waves of the sea became quiet. Then they were
glad because the sea became quiet. And He led
them to the safe place they wanted.

PSALM 107:22–23, 25–30 NLV

When I go out on my own, I usually end up exhausted just when I need the most strength. That's
when I finally realize I've left You out of my boat,
Lord. I cry to You, and You come to my rescue.
You stop the wind and the waves. In the quiet, I
hear Your voice. I'm overwhelmed with gladness.
My heart regains strength. And You lead me to
the exact place I'd been heading all along. Thank
You, Lord, for always being there for me, helping
me, rescuing me, delivering me. Amen.

Thirsting for God's Voice

*Wait and listen, everyone who is thirsty! Come
to the waters; and he who has no money, come,
buy and eat! Yes, come, buy [priceless, spiritual]
wine and milk without money and without price
[simply for the self-surrender that accepts the
blessing]. Why do you spend your money for that
which is not bread, and your earnings for what
does not satisfy? Hearken diligently to Me, and
eat what is good, and let your soul delight itself
in fatness [the profuseness of spiritual joy].*
ISAIAH 55:1–2 AMPC

Lord, I am so ready to drink from Your well of
wisdom. There are so many voices out there,
telling me what is right and what is wrong, what I
should do and what I shouldn't do. Help me, Lord,
to silence the words—written and spoken—of
others that are ringing through my head. Give
me the power and strength to focus on Yours
alone. What You have within Your Book is the
wisdom I crave. Show me what You would have
me read. Then open the doors of my mind so that
I can comprehend what You're telling me. Give
my soul the joy and delight of Your direction! In
Jesus' name, I pray, amen.

Roots in Reality

Every time you cross my mind, I break out in exclamations of thanks to God. Each exclamation is a trigger to prayer. I find myself praying for you with a glad heart. . . . There has never been the slightest doubt in my mind that the God who started this great work in you would keep at it and bring it to a flourishing finish. . . . It's not at all fanciful for me to think this way about you. My prayers and hopes have deep roots in reality.

PHILIPPIANS 1:3–4, 6–7 MSG

❧

So many "things" go through my mind in one day, one hour, one minute, one second, Lord. And sometimes I never stop to dwell on any of them. I just keep focused on the task before me. Yet in doing that, Lord, I can miss Your prompts to pray for someone. So, Lord, help me break out in joyful recognition when someone crosses my mind. Allow that face or name to trigger a prayer on his or her behalf. May I pray that whatever You've begun in that individual will flourish. For prayers aren't just empty incantations—they change reality! In Jesus' name, amen!

Mind Exchange

Incline your ear [submit and consent to the divine will] and come to Me; hear, and your soul will revive. . . . Seek, inquire for, and require the Lord while He may be found [claiming Him by necessity and by right]; call upon Him while He is near. . . . For My thoughts are not your thoughts, neither are your ways My ways, says the Lord. . . . You shall go out. . .with joy and be led forth [by your Leader, the Lord Himself, and His word] with peace.
ISAIAH 55:3, 6, 8, 12 AMPC

Help me to readjust my ears so that I can pick up on Your wavelength, Lord. I'm drawing near to You, waiting and wanting to hear what You have to say. Refresh my soul, Lord, with Your Word as I seek Your face while You're so near to me. I'm calling out to You, emptying my own mind of its constant dialogue so that I can actually *hear* Your voice and exchange my thoughts for Yours, which are always so far above me yet penetrate deep into my own heart. For when I tap into Your wisdom and love, I find myself tasting Your joy and being led, not just by Your peace, but by You Yourself! Amen.

Happy in Faith

Because of your prayers and the help the Holy Spirit
gives me, all of this will turn out for good. . . .
To me, living means having Christ. To die means
that I would have more of Him. If I keep on living
here in this body, it means that I can lead more peo-
ple to Christ. . . . I have a desire to leave this world
to be with Christ, which is much better. But it is
more important for you that I stay. I am sure I will
live to help you grow and be happy in your faith.
PHILIPPIANS 1:19, 21–25 NLV

Some days, Lord, life can be so hard that I just
want You to beam me up. To lift up every part
of me into heaven with You. Yet I know You
have plans for me that are for my good and Your
purpose. So help me to be happy wherever I am,
Lord, in heaven or on earth. Remind me that
things will, in the end, always turn out for good.
Show me, Lord, whom You would have me help
and whom You would have me lead to You so they
can find joy in You. I live to serve You, Lord. In
Jesus' name, amen.

That Middle Ground

*If any person thinks himself to be somebody
[too important to condescend to shoulder another's
load] when he is nobody [of superiority except
in his own estimation], he deceives and deludes
and cheats himself. But let every person carefully
scrutinize and examine and test his own conduct
and his own work. He can then have the personal
satisfaction and joy of doing something commendable
[in itself alone] without [resorting to] boastful
comparison with his neighbor.*

GALATIANS 6:3–4 AMPC

❧

Lord, too often I find myself comparing my work
with that of others. And then I find myself in
one of two places: I'm either not satisfied or too
satisfied with what I've accomplished. If it's the
former, I begin to feel less worthy, less able, less
competent. In other words, I feel less than who
You've made me to be. If it's the latter, I find
myself feeling too worthy, too capable, and too
self-sufficient. Then before I know it, pride has set
in. Help me, Lord, to find that middle ground. To
know that my joy lies in comparing myself with
myself and in doing my work for and in You. That
is my soul reward. In Jesus' name, amen.

Sprouting with Hope

He changes a desert into a pool of water and makes water flow out of dry ground. And He makes the hungry go there. . . . They plant seeds in the fields and plant grape-vines and gather much fruit. He lets good come to them and they become many in number. . . . He lifts those in need out of their troubles. He makes their families grow like flocks. Those who are right see it and are glad.

PSALM 107:35–38, 41–42 NLV

When I'm in a place that seems dry of hope, Lord, I pray to You, and You make water appear out of nowhere. Soon that once-barren landscape within begins to come back to life. You open my eyes to what may be. You urge me to plant seeds of confidence and expectation in You. And soon I'm bearing more fruit than I ever hoped or imagined. Good things begin to sprout up, feeding every part of me—mind, body, spirit, and soul. Once again, Lord, You lift me up out of myself and into You. And I am overcome with gladness, singing with joy. Thank You, Lord, for bringing me back to where You want me to be—joyfully expectant in You. Amen.

The We-Train

Are you strong because you belong to Christ?
Does His love comfort you? Do you have joy
by being as one in sharing the Holy Spirit?
Do you have loving-kindness and pity for each
other? Then give me true joy by thinking the
same thoughts. Keep having the same love. Be as
one in thoughts and actions. . . . Think of other
people as more important than yourself.
PHILIPPIANS 2:1–3 NLV

Lord, I'm back on that all-about-me train. How do I keep getting stuck here? It never leads to happiness, that's for sure. Help me, Lord, to realize that my strength lies is putting others before myself and finding that my joy is tied up with *their* joy. So lead me today, Lord, to be more others- than self-focused. To keep my eyes open to where I can lend a hand or to whom I can lend an ear. Show me to whom You would have me extend a hand of friendship or a word of love. Instead of finding where I am different from another, show me where she and I are the same and can find common ground. Help me get on the we-train and embark upon a joy-meets-joy journey. In Jesus' name, I pray, amen.

Power of the Word

*The rain and snow come down from heaven and
do not return there without giving water to the
earth. This makes plants grow on the earth, and
gives seeds to the planter and bread to the eater.
So My Word which goes from My mouth will not
return to Me empty. It will do what I want it to
do, and will carry out My plan well. You will go
out with joy, and be led out in peace.*

ISAIAH 55:10–12 NLV

❧

The power of Your Word, Lord, is astounding. Just
as the rain and snow You send to earth promote
growth for the fields and food for the farmer, so
does Your Word provide growth and sustenance
in my life. It is food for my soul and water for my
spirit. Your Word carries out Your plan for me
and all Your children. Your promises, so much
stronger than my good intentions, grow me into
the person You want and *need* me to be so that
Your will on earth will be done. In and because
of all this, I am on the path of Your joy, led by
Your peace. In Jesus' name, amen!

Change of Plans

Do not always be thinking about your own plans only. Be happy to know what other people are doing. Think as Christ Jesus thought. Jesus has always been as God is. But He did not hold to His rights as God. He put aside everything that belonged to Him and made Himself the same as a servant who is owned by someone. . . . He gave up His important place.
PHILIPPIANS 2:4–8 NLV

Sometimes, Lord, I tend to get so wrapped up in my own life and plans that I never look around or show any interest in what's happening in the lives of others. Help me to reach out, Lord. I actually want to listen to the plans, dreams, and callings in the lives of others. Help me to put aside what I'd planned for today, even if it's just for a little while, and show an interest in another's ideas. And especially help me, Lord, to be more gracious amid interruptions, recognizing them not as something keeping me from getting what *I* want done that day but as opportunities to do what *You* would have me do to serve You. In Jesus' name, amen.

Shore of God's Desire

When they had rowed three or four miles, they saw Jesus walking on the sea and approaching the boat. And they were afraid (terrified). But Jesus said to them, It is I; be not afraid! [I Am; stop being frightened!] Then they were quite willing and glad for Him to come into the boat. And now the boat went at once to the land they had steered toward. [And immediately they reached the shore toward which they had been slowly making their way.]

JOHN 6:19–21 AMPC

❦

I thank You, Jesus, for always watching out for me. For coming into my life with all Your supernatural strength, with the power You wield to calm the wind and waves that threaten me, within and without. Help me to see You more clearly, Jesus. To recognize You as the Friend and Water-Walker You are. And even more, Lord, make me not just *willing* but *glad* to let You into my boat. For when I do, I know I will be heading the way You want me to go, taking the course Father God planned for me to take. And I will at last find myself reaching the shore of Your desire for me. In Your name, I pray, amen.

Joyful and Obedient

You must keep on working to show you have been saved from the punishment of sin. Be afraid that you may not please God. He is working in you. God is helping you obey Him. God is doing what He wants done in you. Be glad you can do the things you should be doing. Do all things without arguing and talking about how you wish you did not have to do them. In that way, you can prove yourselves to be without blame.

PHILIPPIANS 2:12–15 NLV

Some days I feel like one of the wandering Israelites, Lord. I'm moaning and groaning about all the things I don't want to do. Help me to look at all the blessings in my life instead of at all the seeming curses. For I want to please You, Lord. And no one likes a whiner. Open my eyes to what You are doing within me. Help me not to give up on myself—or You—but recognize that You are helping me follow the path You have purposefully put before me. Make me not stubborn but pliant to Your directions. I want to become the joyful and obedient child You desire, walking in Your way instead of pouting and protesting on the sidelines. In Jesus' name, amen.

Joyful Makeover

*Blessed be the name of the Lord. . . . From
the rising of the sun to the going down of it. . .
the name of the Lord is to be praised! . . . [The
Lord] raises the poor out of the dust and lifts the
needy from the ash heap and the dung hill, that
He may seat them with princes. . . . He makes
the barren woman to be a homemaker and a
joyful mother of [spiritual] children.*

PSALM 113:2–3, 7–9 AMPC

I want to praise You not just in the morning
and evening, Lord, but all the day long! To seek
out the light You send me to guide me throughout my day. To attend to Your whispers, alert to
Your promptings, changing my plans to Yours.
For You are the One who can raise the poor-
est of souls into the richness of heaven. You
are the One with the plan so superior to mine.
Where I have once seen a dead end, a failed
dream, a fading hope, You show me a new road,
a plan that succeeds, and a blazing path forward. You do far more than my limited mind can
even fathom. And in this I find Your joy becomes
mine! Thank You, Abba God! Amen!

Strength to Endure

As you learn more and more how God works,
you will learn how to do your work. We pray
that you'll have the strength to stick it out over
the long haul—not the grim strength of gritting
your teeth but the glory-strength God gives. It is
strength that endures the unendurable and spills
over into joy, thanking the Father who makes
us strong enough to take part in everything
bright and beautiful that he has for us.

COLOSSIANS 1:10–12 MSG

Just when I think I've had it, just when I think
I can endure no more, just when my strength is
gone, You bring me hope. You give me an infusion
of strength and power. And suddenly my desper-
ation has turned into joy! For You have kept me
going, Lord! You have given me the strength to
continue, to get to the place of beauty and joy,
a place I never would have seen had I given up
and dropped out! Thank You, Jesus, for giving
me the faith and power to keep on keeping on
until I reach all things bright and beautiful in
You. Amen.

Living the Life!

*Seize life! Eat bread with gusto, drink wine with
a robust heart. Oh yes—God takes pleasure in
your pleasure! Dress festively every morning.
Don't skimp on colors and scarves. Relish life with
the spouse you love each and every day of your
precarious life. Each day is God's gift. It's all you
get in exchange for the hard work of staying alive.
Make the most of each one! Whatever turns
up, grab it and do it. And heartily!*

ECCLESIASTES 9:7–10 MSG

Lord, I don't want to go through my day as if it's
just one more in the line of many humdrum days
that have gone before it. I want to *seize* this day!
To live as if it might be my last. To enjoy all the
things You have blessed me with—visible and
invisible! I don't want a day to go by without
telling the special people in my life that I love
them, treasure them—and that includes You,
Lord. You are my joy, my Source, my ready and
willing Friend. And I love You more than I ever
thought possible. Help me, Lord, to live this life
to the full, in joy and with passion, making the
most of all the opportunities You lay at my feet.
Amen.

Echoing the Word

When the Message we preached came to you, it wasn't just words. Something happened in you. The Holy Spirit put steel in your convictions. You paid careful attention to the way we lived among you, and determined to live that way yourselves. In imitating us, you imitated the Master. Although great trouble accompanied the Word, you were able to take great joy from the Holy Spirit!—taking the trouble with the joy, the joy with the trouble. . . . Your lives are echoing the Master's Word.

1 Thessalonians 1:5–6, 8 msg

Oh Lord, how wonderful this life is. Day after day, You demonstrate Your love for me. You have chosen me to do something special for You. That's why, when I read Your Word, I become so much a part of it and it becomes so much a part of me. For it prompts Your Spirit to move within me, helping me to live my life as Jesus lived His, to walk in His footsteps and love as He loved. It's to the point that, even though I may suffer at times, I still find my joy in You. Continue to make me and my life an echo of Your Word, from here to heaven and back. Amen.

A Good Place

I cried to the Lord in my trouble, and He. . .
put me in a good place. The Lord is with me.
I will not be afraid of what man can do to me.
The Lord is with me. He is my Helper. . .my
strength and my song. . .the One Who saves
me. The joy of being saved is being heard in the
tents of those who are right and good. The right
hand of the Lord does powerful things.
PSALM 118:5–7, 14–15 NLV

⤙⤙

Lord, I cannot help but sing praises, to be filled
with childlike joy! For when I cry out to You, You
swoop down and lift me up. You put me in a good
place, one where I can catch my breath, see things
anew, regain my hope and strength. Because You
are with me, I need not fear anything! For You are
my Helper, my strength, my song. Because Your
Son has made me good and right in Your eyes,
You will never let me fall. All day long, my joy,
my courage, my blessings are met in the mantra,
"You, Lord, are with me. You, Lord, are with me."
In Jesus' name, amen.

Happy Is She

The Lord says, "Hold on to what is right and fair. Do what is right and good. My saving power will soon come, and I will show what is right. How happy is the man who does this, and the son of man who takes hold of it! How happy is he who keeps the Day of Rest holy, and keeps his hand from doing wrong."

ISAIAH 56:1–2 NLV

❧

This can be a crazy and mixed-up world, Lord. "Doing the right thing" seems to have gone out of style. But You, Lord, have told me what is right and wrong, fair and unfair. In fact, You have left Your Word for me as a guideline and Your Son, Jesus, as an example to follow. So I'm following Your guide and His example. For that is what brings me—and You—joy! Power me up with Your love, Lord, so I can live Your way. Prompt me to cease my work at times, so I can get the rest I need, be renewed in Your strength and light, and find the power to resist a world that wants me to go another way. I'm walking *Your* path, Lord, from here to eternity. In Jesus' name, amen.

A New Day

This is the day that the Lord has made.
Let us be full of joy and be glad in it. O Lord,
we beg You to save us! O Lord, we ask that
You let everything go well for us! Great and
honored is he who comes in the name of the Lord.
We honor you from the house of the Lord.
The Lord is God. He has given us light.

PSALM 118:24–27 NLV

Good morning, Glory! I'm ready to rise and shine! For this is a new day, one You have made. You've set the sun in the sky, the moon in the shadows, and the stars behind Your heavenly blue. Today I am going to be full of joy—for You have brought me a clean slate, a new place to start. I have no idea of all the blessings You have waiting for me, but I am ready to begin by praising You. Today I will focus on all the good around me. I'll be keeping my eyes open to the opportunities that wait just around the corner. Shine Your light upon my path today, Lord. Give me success in all I do. And I will honor You every moment of this day as I walk Your way. Amen.

Joy in Prayer

"As for the outsiders who now follow me, working for me, loving my name, and wanting to be my servants—all who keep Sabbath and don't defile it, holding fast to my covenant—I'll bring them to my holy mountain and give them joy in my house of prayer. They'll be welcome to worship the same as the 'insiders.' . . . My house of worship will be known as a house of prayer for all people."

ISAIAH 56:6–8 MSG

❧

When I first found You, Lord, I felt like an outsider. But as I learned more about You and spent more time in Your Word, I began to feel like an insider. I want to please You, to serve You in every way. I will rest as You bid me rest. Work as You bid me work. Love as You bid me love. Serve as You bid me serve. I thank You for loving me, wanting me, pulling me to You, and bringing me to Your holy mountain. As I enter into Your house, bringing my prayers and praises to You, lying down at Your feet, I will find the joy You so readily promise in that process. In Jesus' name, amen.

The Doer of Great Things

When the Lord brought back the captives [who returned] to Zion, we were like those who dream [it seemed so unreal]. Then were our mouths filled with laughter, and our tongues with singing. Then they said among the nations, The Lord has done great things for them. The Lord has done great things for us! We are glad!

PSALM 126:1–3 AMPC

❧

I am amazed at the mercy You show me, Lord. The way You keep standing with me, loving me, working in me. You never give up. Just when I seem the most irredeemable, You somehow redeem me. Just when I'm the most careless with my life, You take the most care of me. You have said that You will never leave nor forsake me. That I can never be taken out of Your hand. I thank You, Lord, for that, for continually bringing me back to You, for doing wonderful, awe-inspiring things for me. You are a dream come true. You fill my mouth with laughter, my heart with joy. And I, Father, am eternally grateful. In Jesus' name, I pray and say, amen.

A Harbinger of Love

I always thank God when I speak of you in my prayers. It is because I hear of your love and trust in the Lord Jesus and in all the Christians. I pray that our faith together will help you know all the good things you have through Christ Jesus. Your love has given me much joy and comfort. The hearts of the Christians have been made happy by you.

PHILEMON 1:4–7 NLV

Lord, thank You for the love You have poured out upon me. Thank You for its power, how it can never be quenched (see Song of Solomon 8:7). How, even when compared with faith and hope, love is the greatest. Nothing—living or dead, from heaven or hell, from now or tomorrow, high or low, thinkable or unthinkable—can separate Your love from me. Show me in my life, Lord, whom I can love, care for, or comfort as an extension of Your love. For in doing so, I know I will be making another's burden lighter or another's day brighter. Help me, Lord, to be a child of Your love, one who cannot help but share her joy of that love and so bring joy to someone else's heart. Amen.

God's Resting Place

*Let us go into His tabernacle; let us worship
at His footstool. Arise, O Lord, to Your
resting-place, You and the ark [the symbol] of
Your strength. Let Your priests be clothed with
righteousness (right living and right standing with
God); and let Your saints shout for joy! . . .
This is My resting-place forever [says the Lord];
here will I dwell, for I have desired it.*

PSALM 132:7–9, 14 AMPC

Out of all the places You could have chosen to
live, Lord, You decided to live in me. It makes me
reel in wonder that I, this fragile and flawed vessel,
am where You reside. Your strength and power
are within me. Through me, You can change the
world, by little and great words and deeds. Keep
me mindful of this reality, Lord. Help me to step
aside so You can work, pouring out Your light
and love. Show me the way You would have me
direct my feet so that I am where You would have
me be. I know You have a plan, Lord. And I am
amazed and overjoyed that I am part of that plan.
Help me rest in You as You rest in me. In Jesus'
name, I pray, amen.

A Soft Heart

*Christ (the Messiah) was faithful over His
[own Father's] house as a Son [and Master of it].
And it is we who are [now members] of this
house, if we hold fast and firm to the end our
joyful and exultant confidence and sense of
triumph in our hope [in Christ]. Therefore,
as the Holy Spirit says: Today, if you will
hear His voice, do not harden your hearts.*
HEBREWS 3:6–8 AMPC

I admit, Lord, that some days I may not be as
open to You as I should be. I'm so focused on
getting through my earthly tasks that I forget
about my heavenly mission. Or I hear Your voice
but harden my heart against it. I brush it aside,
figuring that if I have time later in my day, then
I'll respond to what You would have me say or do.
At other times, Lord, fear keeps me from going
down the path You'd have me tread. So help me
to have an eager ear and a soft heart where You
are concerned, Lord. To hold fast to my hope
and expectation of Jesus in this life and beyond.
Give me the will, means, courage, and openness
to joyfully do what You desire, no matter when
and no matter how. Amen.

Renewal

Turn to freedom our captivity and restore
our fortunes, O Lord, as the streams in the
South (the Negeb) [are restored by the torrents].
They who sow in tears shall reap in joy and
singing. He who goes forth bearing seed and
weeping [at needing his precious supply of grain
for sowing] shall doubtless come again with
rejoicing, bringing his sheaves with him.
PSALM 126:4–6 AMPC

Only You, Lord, can turn my life around. Only You can make me free again. Only You can restore what I once was or had. So I ask You to do that today, Lord. Turn my tears of sorrow into tears of joy. Remind me of all You have done in my life in the past, all the miracles You have worked, all the ways You have spoken into my heart. I am in need of Your comfort, Lord. I long for the joy I once had. I'm reaching out for the love that has saved me, bringing me back from the brink time and time again. Your having renewed me in the past gives me so much hope in this present moment. I'm already feeling the light of Your presence breaking through my clouds of sorrow. Lift me up with You, Lord, as I rejoice in You anew! Amen.

Rise and Shine!

*Arise [from the depression and prostration in which
circumstances have kept you—rise to a new life]!
Shine (be radiant with the glory of the Lord), for
your light has come, and the glory of the Lord has
risen upon you! For behold, darkness shall cover
the earth, and dense darkness [all] peoples, but the
Lord shall arise upon you. . .and His glory shall be
seen on you. And nations shall come to your light.*
ISAIAH 60:1–3 AMPC

Some days, Lord, I find myself so weighed down
by life, by circumstances, and by the world around
me that I find it hard to get out of bed. I just want
to bury myself beneath the covers and wait for the
tide to turn. That's when I realize I'm losing sight
of Your light, Your command to rise and shine.
So enter into me in a powerful way today, Lord.
Fill me with the glory of Your light. Renew my
faith. Pull me back into the right reality—Your
reality—Your world of joy, love, power, gladness,
and thanksgiving. Come to me, Lord. Brighten
my spirit so I can once more be glad and reflect
the light of Your Son! In His name, amen.

Joy along the Way

Let us put every thing out of our lives that keeps us from doing what we should. Let us keep running in the race that God has planned for us. Let us keep looking to Jesus. Our faith comes from Him and He is the One Who makes it perfect. He did not give up when He had to suffer shame and die on a cross. He knew of the joy that would be His later. Now He is sitting at the right side of God.
HEBREWS 12:1–2 NLV

❧

God, I don't want to give up as I travel with You through this amazing journey called the Way. So help me get rid of anything in my life that keeps me from doing what Your Word would have me do. Help me keep going on this path You have carved out for me. Help me to keep my focus on Jesus and not the winds of adversity. For He is the One who keeps me going, who has the power over all things and makes my path straight, right, and good. Just as He suffered to get to the joy that was His, help me to keep going, knowing that I too will one day be in heaven, rejoicing with Him! Amen.

Big and Small

In the day when I called, You answered me;
and You strengthened me with strength (might and
inflexibility to temptation) in my inner self. . . .
Sing of the ways of the Lord and joyfully celebrate
His mighty acts, for great is the glory of the Lord.
For though the Lord is high, yet has He respect to
the lowly [bringing them into fellowship with Him].
. . . Though I walk in the midst of trouble, You
will revive me; You will stretch forth Your hand.
PSALM 138:3, 5–7 AMPC

It's almost unfathomable, unimaginable, Lord, that You, who created the world and hold boundless power, love, and the destiny of one and all, take notice of me. My life is just a blip on Your map of eternity. Yet You care about me and everything that's happening in my life. So continue to answer my pleas and prayers, Lord. Strengthen me with all the might I need— within and without. Revive me amid troubles, big and small. Stretch forth Your hand to help. Hold me as I sing with joy about all that You have done, will do, and are doing in me! Amen.

Full Play

Consider it wholly joyful, my brethren, whenever
you are enveloped in or encounter trials of any
sort or fall into various temptations. Be assured
and understand that the trial and proving of your
faith bring out endurance and steadfastness and
patience. But let endurance and steadfastness and
patience have full play and do a thorough work,
so that you may be [people] perfectly and fully
developed [with no defects], lacking in nothing.

JAMES 1:2–4 AMPC

This is the joy I'd like to develop, Lord—joy that I can have even in the midst of trials, troubles, and temptations. Help me understand that everything I go through will make me stronger in my faith and increase my patience, endurance, and constancy in You. I realize all this comes to me so that I might be fully developed, strong, complete, and lacking nothing. Yet still, it can be difficult. So please, Lord, give me Your grace and love, Your blessings and peace as I continue on. Help me fully realize Your presence so that I can find Your joy in each and every situation. In Jesus' name, amen.

A New Song

Praise the Lord! Sing to the Lord a new song. . . !
Let Israel rejoice in Him, their Maker; let Zion's
children triumph and be joyful in their King! . . .
For the Lord takes pleasure in His people; He will
beautify the humble with salvation and adorn the
wretched with victory. Let the saints be joyful in
the glory and beauty [which God confers upon
them]; let them sing for joy upon their beds.
PSALM 149:1–2, 4–5 AMPC

Once again, Lord, I cannot help but be amazed
that You take pleasure in my company! That You
actually love when I come into Your presence,
knowing that I'm by no means perfect yet over-
looking that because You see me through the light
and love of Jesus! This fills me with joy, Lord! It
makes me so happy that You long to adorn me
with beauty and glory. That where I see myself as
weak, You see me full of strength. That where I
see myself as lacking, You see me as having it all.
Help me to see me as You see me, Lord, so that I
will have the confidence to do what You would
have me do and to be the joy-filled woman You
designed me to be. Amen!

Times Tested

*Dear friends, your faith is going to be tested
as if it were going through fire. Do not be
surprised at this. Be happy that you are able to
share some of the suffering of Christ. When
His shining-greatness is shown, you will be filled
with much joy. If men speak bad of you because
you are a Christian, you will be happy because the
Spirit of shining-greatness and of God is in you.*

1 Peter 4:12–14 NLV

❧

These days, Lord, many people don't see the virtue of goodness, of following You. In fact, being a Christian seems to have a new connotation—and it's not deemed very positive at all! Your people are being tested, Lord. And amid these tests, I need Your power. I need Your strength to face those who malign me—and You! Help me not to be discouraged but to be encouraged, knowing that Jesus suffered too. He also was shamed and abused. And He came out smelling like a rose on the other side. Help me to do the same, Lord. To keep the joy of You in my heart and mind as You reside within me every step of the way! Amen.

Radiant Light

*Then you shall see and be radiant, and your
heart shall thrill and tremble with joy [at the
glorious deliverance] and be enlarged. . . . The
sun shall no more be your light by day, nor for
brightness shall the moon give light to you, but the
Lord shall be to you an everlasting light, and your
God your glory and your beauty. Your sun shall
no more go down, nor shall your moon withdraw
itself, for the Lord shall be your everlasting light,
and the days of your mourning shall be ended.*
ISAIAH 60:5, 19–20 AMPC

How wonderful, Lord, that someday this world
will be different. That I will have the peace, joy,
and honor that You have promised. That I'll no
longer need the light of the sun or of the moon.
For I'll be walking in *Your* light day and night. I'll
witness Your glory and Your beauty. And sorrow
will be no more. What comfort and joy that brings
me today, Lord, knowing that someday tears will
no longer flow. Thank You, Father God, for the
promise of this day. I tremble with joy in anticipation of what You have in store for those who
love You. In Jesus' name, amen.

Spreading the Word

Christ Who is Life was shown to us. We saw
Him. We tell you and preach about the Life
that lasts forever. He was with the Father and
He has come down to us. We are preaching what
we have heard and seen. We want you to share
together with us what we have with the Father
and with His Son, Jesus Christ. We are writing
this to you so our joy may be full.

1 JOHN 1:2–4 NLV

❧

I can't imagine, Jesus, what it might have been like for Your followers to actually see, touch, and hear You. They could watch You, walk right beside You, or eat dinner with You. Yet what's even more amazing is that You and Your name live on. You knew people would be coming to You thousands of years after You passed into heaven. You made a way for me to follow You. And others wrote about You so that I could find my way and have the joy they had when they saw You face-to-face! I thank You, Jesus, for breathing Your Spirit into others so they would be inspired to spread not just Your Word but the joy of being in You. In Your name, I pray, amen.

The Change Up

*The Lord has chosen me to bring good news to
poor people. . .to heal those with a sad heart. . .
to tell those who are being held and those in prison
that they can go free. . . . He has sent me to
comfort all who are filled with sorrow. . . . I will
give them a crown of beauty instead of ashes. . .
the oil of joy instead of sorrow, and a spirit of
praise instead of a spirit of no hope.*

ISAIAH 61:1–3 NLV

***

You, Lord, are constantly changing things up in
my life. First You brought me the good news of
Your Son, making me feel richly blessed. Then You
made Your way into my heart. And every time I
plant myself in Your Word, I find You continuing
to turn me around. You bring me comfort when
I'm down. You lift my soul from the trappings of
this world so that I can be free once more. Out
of a pile of ashes, You find me roses. When I feel
hopeless, You plant a spirit of praise within me.
Continue to change me, Lord. I want to let You
turn my life around. Amen.

New Day

*I saw Holy Jerusalem, new-created, descending
resplendent out of Heaven. . . . I heard a voice
thunder from the Throne: "Look! Look! God
has moved into the neighborhood, making his
home with men and women! They're his people,
he's their God. He'll wipe every tear from their
eyes. Death is gone for good—tears gone, crying
gone, pain gone—all the first order of things gone."
The Enthroned continued, "Look! I'm making
everything new. Write it all down—each
word dependable and accurate."*

REVELATION 21:2–5 MSG

Oh Lord, how I long for the day when the New
Jerusalem will be my home. When You will have
moved into my neighborhood, making Your home
among all those who have been faithful to You.
For then there will be no pain and no need for
tears. You will be making everything new—even
better than the garden of Eden. This is the hope
I cling to, the thought that gives me so much joy
in this world. For each day is a day to make things
new, to let go of my troubles and melt into You.
Thank You, Lord, for gifting me this present day
that bears the hope of tomorrow with You. In
Jesus' name, amen.

Even Stronger

Pure gold put in the fire comes out of it proved pure; genuine faith put through this suffering comes out proved genuine. When Jesus wraps this all up, it's your faith, not your gold, that God will have on display as evidence of his victory. You never saw him, yet you love him. You still don't see him, yet you trust him—with laughter and singing. Because you kept on believing, you'll get what you're looking forward to: total salvation.

1 Peter 1:7–9 msg

Even when I'm having trouble in my life, Jesus, there's one thing that keeps me going: You. Knowing You are with me. Knowing You walked a much harder road than I am now on and managed, with every test, to come out stronger on the other side. Jesus, although I have never actually seen You, I know You are here. You are the One I can trust. Your promises are what I can hope in. With You by my side and Your Word written in my heart and echoing in my mind, I can face anything with joy and laughter. In Your name, amen!

Teachings

*I am happy to find some of your children
living in the truth as the Father has said we
should. . . . Anyone who goes too far and does
not live by the teachings of Christ does not have
God. If you live by what Christ taught, you have
both the Father and the Son. . . . I hope to come
to you soon. Then we can talk about these
things together that your joy may be full.*

2 JOHN 1:4, 9, 12 NLV

❧

Lord, I want to please You, beyond any church
doctrine or tradition. I want to follow You and
Your teachings—not my own idea of what is right
and wrong. To walk just as Your Word outlines
for me. Yet I don't want to run ahead of what
You would have me be, say, or do. So, Lord Jesus,
reveal to me what You would have me know.
Teach me the right way to live. For when I understand Your truth, I know I'll be walking God's
way. And that's the only right way. In Your path
is where all my joy, strength, hope, and rest lie.
Guide me, Lord. Teach me Your wisdom; show
me Your path from here to eternity. Amen.

The Light

The teachers and those who are wise shall shine like the brightness of the firmament, and those who turn many to righteousness (to uprightness and right standing with God) [shall give forth light] like the stars forever and ever. . . . The light of the [uncompromisingly] righteous [is within him— it grows brighter and] rejoices, but the lamp of the wicked [furnishes only a derived, temporary light and] shall be put out shortly.

DANIEL 12:3; PROVERBS 13:9 AMPC

❧

I want to shine for You, Lord. To walk right, in step with You, and to keep on Your pathway. Abba God, Your Son said, "I am the Light of the world. He who follows Me will not be walking in the dark, but will have the Light which is Life" (John 8:12 AMPC). Thank You for allowing Jesus' light in this dark world to reveal more of You. In this moment, Lord, show me Your bright presence. Shine Your light, which overcomes all darkness and banishes the sorrow that comes with it, into me right now. Make me glow for You and then reflect Your light onto others, spreading Your joy and shining forevermore. In Jesus' name, amen.

Well Versed

Your Word have I hid in my heart, that I may not sin against You. Great and honored are You, O Lord. Teach me Your Law. I have told with my lips of all the Laws of Your mouth. I have found as much joy in following Your Law as one finds in much riches. I will think about Your Law and have respect for Your ways. I will be glad in Your Law. I will not forget Your Word.

PSALM 119:11–16 NLV

❧

Your Word, Lord, is such a treasure. There is nothing I value more, nothing that gives me more hope and joy than hearing and understanding You and Your Word. Teach me what I need to learn today. Help me hide all my knowledge of You within my most sacred place. Then in times of trouble or challenge, I'll have a reserve of Your wisdom that I can pull from to regain my confidence, courage, and joy. Mark out the reading path You would have me take. Show me the words You would have me write upon my heart so that I will be well versed when I need their power. In Jesus' name, amen.

Spiritual Mothers

*I remember you night and day in my prayers,
and. . .as I recall your tears, I yearn to see
you so that I may be filled with joy. I am calling
up memories of your sincere and unqualified faith
(the leaning of your entire personality on God in
Christ in absolute trust and confidence in His
power, wisdom, and goodness), [a faith] that
first lived permanently in [the heart of] your
grandmother Lois and your mother Eunice and
now, I am [fully] persuaded, [dwells] in you also.*

2 TIMOTHY 1:3–5 AMPC

When I think back on all the women in my life
who've helped me find my way to You, Lord,
I cannot help but wonder how You've worked
through them. Because of these spiritual mothers
and grandmothers, I have a faith that brings me
such joy and comfort. For they started me on
the right road, helping me find a way to trust
You and have confidence in You, Your power,
and Your wisdom. Now help me, Lord, to pay
forward the joys and blessings of knowing You.
Help me become a spiritual mother to others.
Show me whom I can help train up or support. Then give me the wisdom and courage to
speak to her, heart-to-heart. Amen.

A Joyful Celebration

*Relax, everything's going to be all right; rest,
everything's coming together; open your hearts,
love is on the way! . . . Carefully build yourselves
up in this most holy faith by praying in the Holy
Spirit, staying right at the center of God's love,
keeping your arms open and outstretched, ready
for the mercy of our Master, Jesus Christ. This
is the unending life, the real life! . . . And now to
him who can keep you on your feet. . .fresh and
celebrating. . .be glory, majesty, strength, and rule.*
JUDE 1:2, 20–21, 24 MSG

❦

I want to build my faith in You, Lord, so that I
no longer get caught up in the tears, pain, and
sorrows of this world and forget about all the hope
I have in You. So give me Your peace, Lord. Remind me all is and will be okay. Give me the rest
I need each day. Help me open my heart, praying
in the Spirit and residing in Your presence and
love. I'm keeping my arms wide open for You,
ready to receive and return Your love. Keep me
on my feet, Lord, standing strong as You lead me
in a joyful celebration of this magnificent life of
faith! Amen.

Queen of the Hill

*Though the cherry trees don't blossom and the
strawberries don't ripen, though the apples are
worm-eaten and the wheat fields stunted, though
the sheep pens are sheepless and the cattle barns
empty, I'm singing joyful praise to GOD. I'm
turning cartwheels of joy to my Savior God.
Counting on GOD's Rule to prevail, I take
heart and gain strength. I run like a deer.
I feel like I'm king of the mountain!*
HABAKKUK 3:17–19 MSG

Lord, no matter how things are going in my life,
no matter how many troubles or trials assail me,
I will continue to trust You. Because that's where
my joy lies. My confidence in You is what keeps
me going merrily along, singing joyful praises to
You and Your name! Even amid loss, I trust You to
keep me whole and hearty, pleased and pleasant.
I'm gaining my strength in You. You are the One
who will give me the power to keep on going, to
step out of my comfort zone and into Your plan
for my life. Even when others are struck low, I'll
be standing sure-footed on Your mountaintop,
queen of the hill with the Lord of love. Amen.

Unbroken Tranquility

*When the Lamb broke the seventh lock, there was
not a sound in heaven for about one-half hour.
Then I saw the seven angels standing before God.
They were given seven horns. Another angel
came and stood at the altar. He held a cup made of
gold full of special perfume. He was given much
perfume so he could mix it in with the prayers of
those who belonged to God. Their prayers were
put on the altar made of gold before the throne.*

REVELATION 8:1–3 NLV

↬

There is something so precious, Lord, about being in silence before You. For in this stillness, I find unbroken tranquility. A time to reflect on the awesomeness of the joy experienced in Your presence. Here I feel Your light, the warmth of Your love and compassion, Your mercy and comfort. It is here, in these unbroken moments with You, that I sit in wonder and anticipation, not knowing what to expect, yet expecting nothing but good. Your peace calms my heart, soul, spirit, body, and mind. Time stands still as I stand with You. Then, little by little, my prayers and praises rise up to You. And I find Your heavenly joy. In Jesus' name, I await. Amen.

One Call Away

" 'Call to me and I will answer you. I'll tell you
marvelous and wondrous things that you could
never figure out on your own.' . . . Working
a true healing inside and out. . .life brimming
with blessings. I'll restore everything that was
lost. . . . I'll build everything back as good as
new. . . . [It] will be a center of joy and praise."
JEREMIAH 33:3, 6–7, 9 MSG

When things look irredeemable and dark, when all
seems lost, I have one hope, Lord: You. You have
said that if I call out to You, You'll hear and answer
me. You'll tell me all kinds of things I don't know.
You'll explain all the mysteries, tell me things I
could never figure out in my own finite mind.
And then You'll fix what seems unfixable. You'll
heal my life, my world, from the inside out. My
life will be running over with so many blessings.
You'll bring back everything I've lost, make my
world as good as new. Because of that promise, I
have hope that my joy and praises to You are one
call away. In Jesus' name, amen.

The Holy Takeover

My grace is enough; it's all you need. My strength comes into its own in your weakness. Once I heard that, I was glad to let it happen. I quit focusing on the handicap and began appreciating the gift. It was a case of Christ's strength moving in on my weakness. Now I take limitations in stride, and with good cheer, these limitations that cut me down to size—abuse, accidents, opposition, bad breaks. I just let Christ take over! And so the weaker I get, the stronger I become.
2 Corinthians 12:9–10 MSG

❧

Lord, You certainly have a way of turning my life upside down. When I'm feeling weak because of some calamity, illness, abuse, or a "bad break," You come out in full force. As I become weaker and weaker, unable to handle things on my own, You show up in a big way and work through me. In fact, You make things perfect! So I'm making a point to stop focusing on what's wrong and to start focusing on You. I'm going to stay joyful no matter what limitations assail me. I'm going to step aside and let *You* take over. In that way, the weaker I get, the stronger in You I'll become. Amen.

News Bearer

*How beautiful on the mountains are the feet
of him who brings good news, who tells of peace
and brings good news of happiness, who tells of
saving power, and says to Zion, "Your God rules!"
. . . You will not go out in a hurry. You will not
leave as if you were running for your lives.
For the Lord will go before you. And the God
of Israel will keep watch behind you.*

ISAIAH 52:7, 12 NLV

I've heard Your Good News, Lord. I've heard of Your Son's strength, peace, love, and saving power. Now, Lord, make me a messenger of Your Good News. Make me a light that helps others find their way to You, the God of all, the King who reigns over all. And as I continue to make my way to You, to walk down the path You have put before me, I will not hurry. For I am confident You are going before me, paving my way. And You are walking behind me, guarding me from the rear. Lord, make my feet beautiful for You as I spread Your joy and share Your news with all. Amen.

Something Better

You had loving-pity for those who were in prison. You had joy when your things were taken away from you. For you knew you would have something better in heaven which would last forever. Do not throw away your trust, for your reward will be great. You must be willing to wait without giving up. After you have done what God wants you to do, God will give you what He promised you.
HEBREWS 10:34–36 NLV

There are times, Lord, when I fear my heart is more attached to the treasures I have on earth than those I have in heaven. Help me change that up, Lord. Help me to have love for people, not things. To be happy whether I have little or lots. To have joy even during times of loss, knowing something better than "things" awaits me in heaven. Also, Lord, give me the patience to wait for You to move in my life and the power to do what You would have me do. For when I'm walking Your way, I know that the fulfillment of the promises You've made to me will follow. Amen.

The Treasured Word

*I would have been lost in my troubles if Your Law
had not been my joy. I will never forget Your Word
for by it You have given me new life. I am Yours.
Save me, for I have looked to Your Law. . . . You
are my hiding place and my battle-covering. I put
my hope in Your Word. . . . I am made happy by
Your Word, like one who finds great riches.*

Psalm 119:92–94, 114, 162 nlv

Lord, when I'm desperate, when I see no way out
of my problems, when I'm overwhelmed with
sorrow, I seek You and Your Word. Save me, Lord.
Be my hiding place. Cover me with Your shadow
so that I can rest and recover. Then, when I can
once again rise in Your power, show me the way
out, the way back to the joy that Your pathway
and presence bring. I am Yours, Lord. All my hope
lies in You and Your wisdom. I come to You lost,
and by Your Word I'm found. Your Word is the
treasure I seek, and it holds the promises of all
my tomorrows. Word by word, I find my peace
and my way back to You. In Jesus' name, amen.

In Your Midst

The King of Israel, even the Lord [Himself],
is in the midst of you. . . . Fear not. . . . Let not
your hands sink down or be slow and listless. The
Lord your God is in the midst of you, a Mighty
One, a Savior [Who saves]! He will rejoice over
you with joy; He will rest [in silent satisfaction]
and in His love He will be silent and make no
mention [of past sins, or even recall them];
He will exult over you with singing.
ZEPHANIAH 3:15–17 AMPC

It amazes me, Lord, that You, the King of kings,
the Master Planner, the Lord of Creation, are
right here in my midst. That gives me courage
to face what lies ahead, to step out of my comfort zone. It gives me the strength I need to say
and do what You would have me say and do.
Even more amazing is that You are happy with
me and love me! And when I make a wrong
move or turn from Your way, You will not just forgive me but *forget* my mistakes. In fact, You will
never mention them. All this, Lord, makes me as
joyful in You as You are in me! Amen!

Book on Living

Everything's falling apart on me, God;
put me together again with your Word.
Festoon me with your finest sayings, God;
teach me your holy rules. My life is as close as
my own hands, but I don't forget what you have
revealed. . . . I inherited your book on living;
it's mine forever—what a gift! And how happy it
makes me! I concentrate on doing exactly what
you say—I always have and always will.

PSALM 119:107–109, 111–112 MSG

❧

Just when I feel as if I'm losing my way, Lord, I run to Your Book. Use Your words to put me back together, Lord. To get me back on the right track, living Your way. Teach me what I need to learn so I don't backtrack or take a wrong turn. Help me follow Your rules of life so that I can stop worrying and begin rejoicing! So that I can have the promise of Your peace, love, strength, and power. Help me focus on You and Your way so I won't lose my way to You. And if I do make a mistake, Lord, gently lead me back to You, Your path, Your Son. In His name, amen.

Healing Sun

*Prove Me now by it, says the Lord of hosts, if I
will not open the windows of heaven for you and
pour you out a blessing, that there shall not be
room enough to receive it. . . . Unto you who re-
vere and worshipfully fear My name shall the Sun
of Righteousness arise with healing in His wings
and His beams, and you shall go forth and gambol
like calves [released] from the stall and leap for joy.*

MALACHI 3:10; 4:2 AMPC

When I give my all to You, Lord, You return to
me so much more. Your blessings are so many and
so massive that I cannot hold them all. On top of
all this, You have allowed Your Son to die for me.
When I am basking in His presence, worshipping
and loving Him, He rises up and heals me. He
takes all my sin stains and makes them white as
snow. He takes all my prayers and turns them
into praises. He takes all my sorrows and replaces
them with joy. Thank You, Lord, for all You have
allowed so that I can dance, sing, and leap for joy
in the Son-shine. In Jesus' name, amen.

Scripture Index

OLD TESTAMENT

Exodus
19:4 147

Deuteronomy
16:10, 14–15 25
33:27 147

1 Samuel
18:5–7 26
30:3–4, 6, 8, 19 20

2 Samuel
5:6–7, 10 21

2 Kings
4:21, 23–26 19

1 Chronicles
4:9–10 18
16:8–12 55
16:26–27, 31–33 61

2 Chronicles
20:15–17 22
20:20–22 23
20:25–27 76
20:27 23

Ezra
3:11–12 102
6:14, 16, 22 27

Nehemiah
2:2, 4–5, 8 108
8:8, 10 5

Esther
5:9 123
8:16–17 123

Job
8:5–7, 20–21 134

Psalms
4:4–8 42
5:3, 11 28
16:1–3 7
16:5–6, 10–11 8
16:7–9 6
21:1–3, 6–7 49
27:1, 5–6 16
27:9–10, 13–14 17
30:1–4 57
30:4–5, 10–12 59
32:1–3, 5 65
32:6–7, 10–11 68
33:1, 4, 8–9, 11–12 71
33:16–17, 20–22 74
37:1–5 10
37:7–9, 11 13
37:23–24, 28, 40 14
40:1 120
40:1–4 125
40:5, 8, 16–17 128
40:16 147

43:3–5. 78
47:1–4, 8. 83
48:2–3, 9, 14. 85
51:1, 4, 7–8, 10. 94
51:10–12, 14. 98
63:1–2, 4–5. 90
63:3, 6–8, 11. 96
65:1–4, 8. 92
65:9–13. 100
66:1, 5–6, 12, 20. 104
71:3, 17–18, 20, 23. 44
81:1, 7, 10, 13 106
84:1–3. 110
84:4–7. 113
84:8–12. 115
89:15–18. 121
91:1–2, 4–5, 11. 130
92:1–2, 4, 11–14. 132
97:9–12. 47
107:4–7, 9, 22. 139
107:10–11, 13–14, 22. 143
107:17–20, 22. 149
107:22–23, 25–30. 154
107:35–38, 41–42. 160
113:2–3, 7–9. 166
118:5–7, 14–15. 170
118:24–27. 172
119:11–16. 192
119:92–94, 114, 162. 201
119:107–109, 111–112. . . . 203
126:1–3. 174
126:4–6. 178
132:7–9, 14. 176
138:3, 5–7. 181
149:1–2, 4–5. 183

Proverbs

3:5–8, 13. 51
3:13–18. 63
12:20, 22, 25, 28 81
13:9 191

14:10, 26, 30, 33 117
15:4, 23, 28, 30 29
15:13, 15–16. 30
21:3, 15, 21, 31 135
30:7–9. 138

Ecclesiastes

2:24–26. 69
3:1–4. 73
5:18–20. 86
8:12–15. 144
9:7–10. 168

Song of Solomon

2:3–4, 6. 31
2:13–15. 32
5:2–3. 33
7:10 34
7:10–11. 120
8:1, 3 147
8:7, 14 34

Isaiah

9:1–3, 6. 79
26:3–4, 19. 146
30:18 11
35:3–6. 150
49:13, 15–16. 45
51:1–3. 53
52:7, 12 199
53:3 39
55:1–2. 155
55:3, 6, 8, 12 157
55:10–12. 162
56:1–2. 171
56:6–8. 173
60:1–3. 179
60:5, 19–20. 185
61:1–3. 187

Jeremiah
15:15–16. 37
29:11–13. 15
33:3, 6–7, 9. 197

Daniel
12:3 191

Joel
2:12–14. 152

Habakkuk
3:17–19. 195

Zephaniah
3:15–17. 202

Malachi
3:10 204
4:2 204

NEW TESTAMENT

Matthew
2:9–12. 64
5:2–3. 36
5:2, 4 39
5:2, 6 43
5:2, 7 46
5:2, 8 50
5:2, 9 52
5:2, 10–11. 54
5:5 41
7:7–8. 9
9:27, 29–30. 46
11:28–30. 66
13:20–21, 23. 67
13:44–46. 75
14:28–31. 126
21:5 41

25:20–21. 72
28:1, 5, 7–9. 77

Luke
1:13–15. 60
1:42, 45–49. 62
2:8–11. 82
7:16–17, 21. 80
10:19–20. 87
10:21, 23 88
15:8–10. 89
15:17–18, 20, 22–23. 91
19:2–6. 93
24:29–32. 95
24:38–41. 97
24:45, 50–52. 99

John
1:18 50
3:28–30. 103
4:31–32. 43
6:19–21. 164
8:12 191
11:34–36. 39
13:5 36
14:1–2, 4. 107
14:16, 18, 23, 27 109
15:5, 7, 11 111
16:20, 23–24. 118
16:21–23. 114
17:12–13, 20. 129
20:19–22. 48
20:26, 29 56
21:3–4, 6, 11. 58

Acts
2:25–26, 28. 131
8:26–27, 29–30, 38–39. . . . 133
12:5–7, 12–14. 136
16:24–26. 140
16:29–31, 34. 141

16:31–34. 142
20:22–24. 148

Romans
5:1–3. 24
5:3–5. 84
12:2, 8–9. 101
12:9–13. 105
12:14–16, 18. 112
14:13, 17–18. 116
15:1–2. 122
15:4–6. 124
15:12–13, 33. 127

2 Corinthians
7:4–7. 145
8:2–5. 151
9:6–8. 70
12:9–10. 198

Galatians
5:13, 16, 22–23. 153
6:3–4. 159

Ephesians
2:13–14. 52

Philippians
1:3–4, 6–7. 156
1:19, 21–25. 158
2:1–3. 161
2:4–8. 163
2:12–15. 165
4:4–7. 35
4:8–9. 38
4:10–13. 40

Colossians
1:10–12. 167

1 Thessalonians
1:5–6, 8. 169

2 Timothy
1:3–5. 193

Philemon
1:4–7. 175

Hebrews
3:6–8. 177
10:34–36. 200
12:1–2. 180

James
1:2–4. 182
1:5–8. 12

1 Peter
1:7–9. 189
3:18 54
4:12–14. 184

2 Peter
1:19 120

1 John
1:2–4. 186

2 John
1:4, 9, 12 190

Jude
1:2, 20–21, 24. 194

Revelation
8:1–3. 196
21:2–5. 188